Newmarket Public Library

P9-BAW-971

17.95

ALIENS
The Final Answer?

COPY 1

ALIENS
The Final Answer?

A UFO Cosmology for the 21st Century

DAVID BARCLAY

Newmarket Public Library

BLANDFORD

A BLANDFORD BOOK

First published in the UK 1995
by Blandford
an imprint of Cassell plc
Wellington House,
125 Strand, London WC2R 0BB

Copyright © 1995 David Barclay

The right of David Barclay to be identified as author of this work has been asserted by him in accordance with the provisions of the UK Copyright, Designs and Patents Act 1988.

All rights reserved. No part of this book may be reproduced or transmitted in any form or by any means, electronic or mechanical, including photocopying, recording or any information storage and retrieval system, without permission in writing from the copyright holder and publisher.

Distributed in the United States by Sterling Publishing Co., Inc.
387 Park Avenue South, New York, NY 10016–8810

Distributed in Australia by Capricorn Link (Australia) Pty Ltd
2/13 Carrington Road, Castle Hill, NSW 2154

A Cataloguing-in-Publication Data entry for this title is available from the British Library

ISBN 0–7137–2496–X (hbk)
ISBN 0–7137·2498–6 (pbk)

Typeset by Litho Link Ltd, Welshpool, Powys, UK
Printed and bound in Finland by Werner Söderström Oy

MAY 3 1 1996

Contents

CHAPTER 1
Too Much Monkey Business

I SOMETIMES feel that if I want to see a being which is totally alien to our planetary ecosystem, all I have to do is look in a mirror. We – that is the human race – do not fit comfortably into the ecological matrix of this planet. Yet, this fact seems not to be fully appreciated by those whose chosen brief in life is to derive a sensible cosmology from the, often conflicting, data available. It is possible that, being only human, they sometimes put the demands of scholarly atheism before the requirements of scientific impartiality when considering the evidence that argues for conclusions other than evolution to explain the human presence on Earth. Which is not to say that I fully endorse the Biblical account of humankind's beginnings either; rather I would maintain that there could be another explanation to reconcile the two mutually exclusive scenarios of creationism and evolutionism without actually invalidating either of them. Probably because of this, I am intellectually incapable of under-standing why the idea of the human race being related to monkeys exercises such fascination for the humanist scientific élite; or why the content of Darwin's *Origin of the Species* and *The Descent of Man* took on the attributes of 'Holy Writ' in the way they obviously did, when it was seemingly known from the outset that evolutionary theory was flawed – especially in respect of human-kind's origins and possible evolution from naturally generated mammalian hominid types. Meantime, the real Holy Writ (i.e., Genesis) concerning the origins of our species was devalued and relegated to the status of a phantasmagorical mythology – sundry evolutionists insinuating that Genesis was a kind of pre-scientific fairy-tale that was not undermined until the nineteenth century, when science arrived to set the record straight. Or rather, science replaced a previous unscientific superstition with one more in keeping with ideas about 'technological progress' current at the time, because even today, after years of digging and collecting evidence, palaeontology has signally failed to make the evolutionary case for the genesis of humankind. In fact:

> Despite the identification of some 130,000 fossil specimens, dating back hundreds of millions of years, it is now estimated that the fossil record is 99% incomplete if compared to that which should be expected if evolution is really the accounting mechanism to explain the appearance and ongoing diversity of life on earth.[1]

This cautionary comment must be acknowledged to apply even more stringently in the case of humankind, as in pursuing a coherent answer to the question of the origins of our species there presently seems to be more circumstantial evidence in support of the Biblical 'mythology' regarding this, than there is to put beyond the shadow of a doubt the scientific accuracy of the 'mythology' of evolutionary theory.

Given the intellectual climate of the age that brought forth the notions of a 'Great Machine' Universe, and 'Billiard Ball' atomic theory, it should come as no surprise to learn that the general public has been apparently deceived by a kind of scientific sleight of hand into favouring Darwin's evolutionary explanation of humankind's origins rather than the Biblical version of creation. The reasons for this have more to do with the intellectual inertia bequeathed to us by the overweaning atheism of the steam-driven Victorian scientific mentality than with truly scientific objectivity. So intransigent has been palaeontology's public espousal of humankind's alleged simian ancestry since Darwin's day, it has now somehow become 'politically correct' as scientific fact, while its opponent 'creationism' has disappeared into the realms of 'pre-scientific' superstition. Consequentially, those who still believe in it are castigated as 'fundamentalist' fools. It is palaeontologically implied that the fossil evidence supporting the scientific case is irrefutable. However, the real situation is that 'there is an unbridged gap in the fossil record between ourselves and our presumed ancestor Homo Erectus'.[2] Conventional palaeontology is well aware of this gap in the fossil record, but it chooses to ignore it in favour of *ex cathedra* statements emphasizing evolutionary dogma and, fulfilling the scientific definition of a *myth*, 'presents itself as an authoritative account of the facts, which is not to be questioned, however strange it might seem'.[3] From this, it has to be understood that evolutionism is as much a belief system as creationism. In reality, there is even less evidence to support the claims of Darwinian evolutionary theory than there is to support the claims of creationist theory.

It is a matter of palaeontological record that in Europe there is a distinct gap in the fossil record separating *Homo erectus* from *Homo sapiens*, a gap which is mirrored in the African anthropological record where a skull – at first thought to be that of a fossil gorilla – found at Broken Hill, Zambia, in 1921, was pressed into evolutionary service as some kind of 'link' in the 'evolutionary chain' that, palaeontology devoutly believes, produced ourselves. In alleging that the Broken Hill skull was part of the hypothetical chain that linked *Homo erectus* to modern man, palaeontology patently ignored the fact that this skull – if indeed it was not that of a fossilized gorilla as had been originally thought – actually had features that indicated it was more Neanderthal than near human. The features it displayed were described by Arthur Woodward, an anatomist at the Natural History Museum in London, as follows (according to Brian Fagan in his book, *The Journey From Eden*):

> The skull had massively developed brow ridges over the eye sockets, a flat sloping forehead, and a marked constriction of the skull behind the brow.[4]

Apparently, Arthur the anatomist also pointed out that the face was unusually large and elongated, with a wide palate and 'blown out' cheek-bones. I don't know about you, but to me that does not sound very much like anyone I would care to claim as an ancestor. Perhaps palaeontology ignored the obviously Neanderthal attributes of the skull – and also the fact its owner had lived at the same time as the Neanderthal communities in Europe – because it knew that to have identified the find officially as the skull of a Neanderthal man would have done nothing to close the glaring gap in the evolutionary chain. As it is acknowledged by palaeontology that Neanderthal man did not evolve into Cro-Magnon, it is therefore not part of the hypothetical evolutionary chain that palaeontologists presume produced the present human race.

In view of all this, it now seems only common sense to accept that the genesis of our race is so shrouded in mystery that neither religion nor science is, or has been, able to shed any real light on the subject. The problem is threefold. Firstly, we do exist; so, being finite creatures, and despite our racial evolutionary anomalies that pose problems for conventional palaeontology even without the added embarrassment of being unable to find 'the missing link', we obviously must have had a beginning some time, somewhere. Secondly, we are demonstrably different to all other animals on Earth. In fact, we are not just different, but quantitatively different, in that we are – and up to a point always have been – outside the control of the ecosystem that allegedly 'evolved' us. Thirdly, apart from our escalating technology, we are essentially no different now, physically or mentally, to what we were at our very beginnings. Evolution, it would appear, produced us fully developed. We were 'pre-adapted' (a scientific way of saying 'miraculously prepared') to occupy our present 'niche' – the dominant life form that has taken over our planet and transcended the system that (allegedly) produced it. From this, among much else, it can be deduced that Darwinism works fine on paper, but it is impractical in the field. Evolutionary theory, at least to my mind, relies far too much on the notions of cosmic coincidence and pre-adaptation to be taken too seriously – pre-adaptation being defined as 'the development of a structure in one environment (e.g. lungs in fish) that proves to be of even greater use in another (e.g. on land)'.[5] After all, such arguments in favour of evolution can be seen as only the scientific equivalent of creationist religious miracle-mongering. And even palaeontologists have been known to ask the odd awkward question about how this (unproven yet again) pre-adaptive system would operate in light of the demands of 'survival of the fittest' evolutionary mechanics. For instance, 'What use is a lens in the eye unless it works? A distorting lens might be worse than no lens at all.'[6] How true, but when going on to give a rather specious explanation of how 'half-evolved' attributes might benefit an organism, the poser of the above problem steers well clear of including being half blind in his list of meaningful mutations. So, if evolutionists really want to dispense with God, and so make evolution into an impartial and uncaringly mechanistic 'natural' process, then they must forego the luxury of endowing their hypothetical non-conscious system of 'survival of the fittest' with a God-like capacity for anticipating what the future holds for the life forms it produces, and of then preparing them in advance for whatever eventuality was foreseen. As Wallace, the co-creator with Darwin of the evolutionary hypothesis, wrote: 'Nature never overendows a species beyond the demands of everyday existence.'[7] Relating that to us would inevitably mean that even in prehistory automobiles broke down at the most inconvenient times. So, before proceeding any further, we must realize that there is not only a religious mythology but also a palaeontological mythology to contend with when seeking answers to the mystery that surrounds the genesis of our race. We must also understand that, because there is little to choose between the two mythologies, we must look elsewhere – improbable though it may seem – for clues to answer the where, why, how and when of the origin of our species.

Perhaps it was because Darwin was, after all, merely a 'gifted amateur' (a form of scientific life more prevalent, and influential, in Victorian times than the present) that the idea of our descent from ape-like ancestors appealed so strongly to him. We can only presume that it was because of his inherent amateurism that he was beguiled by his unaided observations to mistake illusion for reality. Similarly, unaided observation of the Sun, Moon and stars apparently going round the Earth provoked and perpetuated the assumption that the Earth was the centre of the Universe. To the untutored eye, apes could convey the impression of being 'less advanced' versions of ourselves, especially with their gift for mimicry, but closer observation would show that this apparent physical similarity is an illusion, and that we have very little in common with primates – not even our chromosome count. For example, we walk upright because our proportions radically differ from simian ones – long legs and short arms, rather than the pongid alternative. Even so-called 'primitive humans' have this same locomotive characteristic. There are no knuckle daggers in the human family, and I would dare to suggest, never were. We also have a truly opposable thumb, and our feet bear very little resemblance to their simian counterpart. Also, we are basically far more savage, individually and – perhaps more importantly –

collectively, than any primate or, indeed, any other mammal. Therefore, it does begin to seem as if the evolutionary mythology is turning out to be merely the atheistic equivalent of Christian fundamentalism, because it is unsupported by any really coherent evidence from the fossil record to show us slowly changing from apedom to manhood over geological time. In all probability, the truth is something else again, and it would behove those who appoint themselves 'Sages of the Ages' to remember that opinion, belief and unsupported speculations are not the same as facts. And the facts are that 'evolution' is a scientific 'fashion' that is as out of place these days as bustles and top hats. Creationism has yet to be scientifically rebutted – only 'debunked' – despite what was implied by Spencer Tracy in the film about the Skopes trial. Strange to say, there is something else that science likes to 'debunk' rather than refute: it is the UFO phenomenon. This might make us wonder if flying saucers might be more closely connected to the mystery of human origins than is the theory of evolution.

Although Charles Darwin was only an 'amateur' scientist, it can be surmised with some confidence that even he must have had his doubts about the applicability of the evolutionary theory to the human race. Without any doubt, the co-creator of the notion of an evolutionary process determined by the dictates of natural selection, Alfred Russell Wallace, had serious reservations in this area and 'finally concluded that Mankind was an exception to the orderly operation of biological laws'.[8] Confirmation that humankind is seen, even by the professionals, as something of an enigma in evolutionary terms is contained in the statement by palaeontologist Oswaldo Reig, 'disregarding the *peculiar phenomenon* of human evolution'.[9] [author's italics]

Such a statement by a palaeontologist must give rise to questions of why human evolution is considered peculiar, and in relation to what – a question that will be answered later to point up something even more peculiar, in evolutionary terms, than the appearance on the world stage of the human race. Suffice it to say for the moment that as natural selection was seen by Wallace as so inappropriate an evolutionary explanation, he had to speculate that 'some intelligent power has guided or determined the development of Mankind'.[10] As it is admitted that Wallace was never convinced that evolution could explain the existence of the human brain, and that he had strong spiritual leanings, could he, therefore, have been considering an 'act of God' (i.e., creation) as a more acceptable alternative to humankind's evolution? The words above seem to point to it. It is almost certain that Darwin himself entertained similar doubts about the feasibility of the evolutionary theory applying to humankind. Because of this, he had apparently admitted:

> His principle of limited perfection – that is, the idea that life could evolve only enough to survive in competition with other life or to adjust to changes in environment – had been oddly upset in the case of Man.[11]

Yet, probably because it was he rather than Wallace who was called upon to be the public champion of their joint theory that Darwin never expressed himself as forcibly in this matter as did Wallace. Although apparently fully aware of all the above, the paucity of the fossil record is glossed over by modern palaeontology in its ongoing efforts not to think the unthinkable: that creation and not evolution is more appropriate to explaining the existence of humankind on Earth. Yet, it still cannot produce the much vaunted 'missing link' that would settle the matter once and for all by irrevocably connecting humankind to *Homo erectus*, and thereby make monkeys of us all.

In its efforts to find fossil evidence of the desired connection to apedom, palaeontology has been compelled, time and again, to revise backwards into geological time its estimates of the length of time humankind has been on the Earth. According to the dictates of Darwin's doctrine as interpreted by the prelates of palaeontology, we, the human race, should be 'johnny-come-latelys' on the planetary stage. If so, what of the sandalled footprints found, in 1968, fossilized in the Cambrian shale at Antelope Springs, Utah? 'One print had a squashed trilobite embedded in it.'[12] If these footprints are accepted by palaeontology, then the crushed trilobite indicates that something resembling modern man a (bi-pedal shoe wearer) was strolling about the Earth 500 million years before humankind supposedly evolved – during the time when the Earth only possessed life in the form of marine invertebrates. That something is drastically wrong with Darwinian evolutionary theory is evinced by the fact that the Antelope

Springs example is but one of many 'fossilized human footprint' anomalies tending to indicate strongly that humankind is, and probably always has been, beyond explanation by a mechanistic evolutionary theory. For instance, 'In 1927, Albert E. Knapp found what appeared to be the fossilized imprint of a shoe sole in limestone of the Triassic Period, near Fisher Canyon in Pershing County, Nevada.'[13] From the same source, many more examples of anomalous footprints could be quoted which strongly indicate that palaentology has more in common with theology than it would care to admit when it comes to defending evolutionary dogma . . . but there's more. Even humankind's alleged 'ancestor', *Homo erectus*, dated by palaeontology to have been living approximately 500,000 years ago, has had to be regressed by over 500,000 years due to finds made at Olduvai Gorge, Tanzania, in 1960. Then, 'In August, 1972, Richard Leakey's young associate Bernard Ngeneo found a shattered cranium in a steep gully in the grey-brown wastelands east of Kenya's Lake Rudolph.'[14] What made this find so damaging to evolutionary theory was the fact that it was identified by Leakey, according to its attributes, as belonging to modern man, which meant that humankind had appeared on the Earth well before the hominid types who should have preceded him in geological time. Furthermore, 'Early in 1975 Dr Stanley Rhine of the University of New Mexico announced his discovery of humanlike footprints in strata indicative of 40 million years old.'[15] Apparently, only a few months previously similar finds had been made in Oklahoma and Wisconsin. Then, to top everything, 'At Glen Rose, Texas, a 16-inch hominid footprint was found next to dinosaur tracks in contemporaneous strata.'[16] This can only mean that humankind and the dinosaurs might well have lived at the same time, which is exactly the point I am trying to make: that most of the evolutionary puzzles relating to humankind would be easily resolved by allowing it to have started the climb to the top of the ecological heap during – or even before – the age of the dinosaurs. Why is that seemingly outside the palaeontological pale? Especially since it is clear that evolutionary efforts that concentrate on the orthodoxy of mammalian hominid evolution have to exclude much relevant data from their deliberations to make even the little headway that they have.

From the foregoing, it is quite clear that evolutionists, in refusing to acknowledge extant evidence which might invalidate evolutionary theory, at least where humankind is concerned, are really only interested in preserving their dogmatism, as were the cardinals of an earlier orthodoxy who refused to look through Galileo's telescope. It has been ever thus: established vested interests always seem to think that if they ignore reality, it won't be there – the ostrich syndrome. However, if archaeology now seems ready to admit that:

> The study of prehistory today is in a state of crisis. Archae-ologists all over the world have realized that much of prehistory, as written in the existing textbooks, is inadequate: some of it is quite simply wrong.[17]

Likewise, palaeontology must take heed of similar shortcomings in its present body of knowledge, and come to terms with the notion that evolution and creation are possibly not mutually exclusive methods in the making of humankind.

In many ways, until we have a more certain date for the appearance of humankind on the Earth, it does not really matter how it was brought into being. The point being made is that humankind existed on Earth during the so-called Age of the Dinosaurs because the creatures that gave rise to them both came from the Age of Reptiles. I know that if this is true, then palaeontology has got its hypotheses wrong somewhere; it is a nonsense that it has to revise its options every time new bones are unearthed. Orthodox evolutionary theory also cannot account for humankind's unique intelligence – unnecessary in terms of survival of the fittest – nor humankind's lack of body hair – anomalous in terms of the rest of anthropoid evolution – and 'why does Mankind display 312 distinctive physical traits that set him utterly apart from his so-called primate cousins?'[18]

In view of all this, one could be forgiven for wondering how Darwin could persist in promulgating so obviously flawed a system. The reason, as already mentioned, was because he was an amateur, who 'did not teach in a University, or work in a labor-atory'.[19] Apparently, most of his ideas derived from his observations while voyaging in the *Beagle*, more specifically, his observations of the fate of the flora and fauna of the Galapagos Islands. Yet, even here no 'advanced' examples of existing species were found; all the animals, despite cosmetic, physical modifications, remained what their kind throughout the world were – just animals. How Darwin derived the evolutionary insight from all this is not clear, because there were no monkeys on the islands. In any case, not only was Darwin an amateur, he had other interests that apparently took precedence over his 'scientific' activities. As his father admonished him, 'You care for nothing but shooting, dogs, and rat catching, and you will be a disgrace to yourself and all your family.'[20] If Darwin's father had said 'the human family', he would have hit it right on the nose. None the less, Darwin's amateurism and 'childlike' enthusiasm can also be called in his defence. However, no such excuses can exonerate the professionals who followed in his footsteps. Their atheistic aim, from first to last, was to use Darwin's delusion to replace religious superstition with an equally insupportable scientific superstition. In effect, they used, and are still using, evolutionary theory to grind their atheistic axes. God knows why! Such scientists are the fossilized remains of Victorian cosmological vanity. It cannot be too strongly stressed that humankind, whatever its real genesis, did not, and demonstrably could not, have 'descended' from an 'ancestor' common to both apes and itself. We are not 'naked apes', probably not even mammals.

Among the above-mentioned '312 physical traits', that argue against humankind's connection with apedom at any point in the geological time scale, there are a couple of physical attributes of humankind that, when taken in conjunction with all the rest, conclusively set it apart from its so-called simian siblings – attributes that argue conclusively for humankind as being unrelated to the apes, and which, in effect, undermine everything that the prelates of the evolutionary anti-religion have thus far told us about ourselves, and our origins. Why palaeontology has been able to propagate and promote the theory of evolution – especially as it applies to humankind – and even to imply strongly that we are not in any way connected to the rest of the mammalian development on this planet, is almost as big a mystery as our real racial origins. The physical attributes regarding our racial physiology are sufficient to silence for ever the evolutionists' claims to our race being a monkey's uncle. The attributes that do more than call into question our simian/hominid/mammalian ancestry have something to do with sex:

Firstly, the human male is unique in that he is the only land roving mammal, the only animal on Earth, able to achieve and maintain an erection without use of a penis bone. His sexual hydraulics are unique to him. Secondly, the human female has a feature unique to herself, the hymen. No other animal has this feature, the sole purpose of which seems to be to indicate the condition known as virginity.[21]

To what purpose I could not say, but I do think it fair to mention that if such anomalous attributes had somehow been deduced from the fossil record regarding an extinct life form, palaeontology would have experienced no difficulty in denying it the mammalian classification. So, why treat a living species any differently? If, as evolutionary theory maintains, humankind is related to the monkey, having evolutionary ancestors in common with them, why are not the aforementioned sexual features apparent in at least one or other of the pongid types? If such features are present in ourselves, they must be considered – in evolutionary terms – as being contributory to successful survival. Therefore, it should be expected that they would feature among other hominid survivor types, such as gorillas or chimps or indeed any one of the 'cousins' which evolutionists claim as our relatives. But they do not, and so call into question the whole of Darwin's carefully constructed, nineteenth-century, pseudo-intellectual, atheistic, evolutionary fantasy.

However, in refusing to accept the unproven dogmas of evolutionary theory, are we then only left with the equally unproven dogmas of creationism? Even if we are unable to accept being the descendants of ape-like ancestors, there are other options open to us before succumbing to spiritual superstition as an antidote for its scientific equivalent. There is, for instance, the argument that our race is the product of a union between the hominid development on Earth and representatives of an extraterrestrial race. This has been argued because there was insufficient geological time available for unaided evolution to have produced our 'big brain' if we only got our racial start in the Age of Mammals – and well into it at that, according to orthodox evolutionists. This 'big brain' every so often, inexplicably produces the phenomenon of 'genius', which is allegedly exclusive to humankind. It is argued that:

> Only great-brained men from extraterrestrial sources could
> have injected those supermind genes into the racial blood-
> stream of mankind on earth. Otherwise, science and biology
> simply have no explanation for genius except to call it a
> 'fortunate' [the old cosmic coincidence, scientific miracle-
> mongering again] mixture of genes and chromosomes but one
> that violates the laws of heredity.[22]

It is flattering to our egos, no doubt, to believe that we, as a race,
are related by blood to some ill-defined but none the less
incredibly intelligent, aliens – almost as ego-inflating as believing
that we are a special creation of some equally ill-defined 'God'.
Once such a notion takes hold, it becomes almost too easy to find
arguments in its favour. Most of them go something like this:

> Up to now, none of our classic theories could satisfactorily
> explain the sudden appearance of the Cro-Magnon man on
> earth. And no one using the classic theories of evolution will
> ever explain how the Cro-Magnon, immediately upon arrival,
> could calculate the Nineveh Constant, based on the planets
> Uranus and Neptune, which he couldn't even see, and the
> imperceptible displacement of the equinoctial point that shifts
> west by only one degree every seventy two years.
> In my opinion, both these mysteries have just one
> explanation – the intervention of astronauts from another
> world.[23]

To attempt such theorizing, one has to subscribe to a kind of
selective evolutionary theory which still accepts that humankind
first appeared on Earth during the Age of Mammals, and that it
was tinkered into its present form by aliens who just happened to
be passing, and no doubt thought it was a good idea at the time.
This kind of reasoning, while a little outré, still manages to keep
our egos intact by maintaining that we are of superior ancestry to
the rest of the mammalian life forms produced by natural
evolution on this planet – which, indeed, we are . . . probably.
But superior in ancestry to every form of life ever produced on
our planet? Well, we shall see.

By every cosmological route we theoretically take, we always
manage to end up arguing for ourselves as the kings of creation.
God, aliens or evolution, it makes no difference who we speculate
called us into existence, we always come out on top . . . in our

own estimation. Yet, there is still one puzzling aspect to our existence which is unanswered by recourse to any of the usual argumentative options. It is one that, when properly understood, will probably puncture our cosmological balloon at the same time as indicating the real reason for our existence. Once again we find that science, in the persona of ethnologists, anthropologists and palaeontologists, stands silent in the face of this evolutionary enigma. To be fair, even theologians have been unable to plumb the mind of God to solve this one; it is this:

> Why is the human race so variegated as to shape, size, skull structure, facial characteristics, and many other anatomical features?
> *Why particularly are there men of varicoloured skin – white, red, yellow, brown and black?*[24]

Granted there are these same differences between extant pongid classes, but the above differences are between different races of beings (i.e., gorillas, orang-utans, etc). The difference with humankind is that all this variegation of the individual is between members of the same race. Contrary to what racialists would have us believe, there *is* only one race of humankind on Earth. This point is proven quite unambiguously by the fact that any human type can produce viable offspring from cohabiting with any other human type. This is in addition to human males and females sharing the anomalous sexual attributes referred to above. All our chromosomes match, ergo we *are* all brothers (and sisters) under the skin. So, with the human race what we actually have is one race with a plethora of variegated 'breeds' – yet another attribute that makes humankind anomalous in nature, but not exactly anomalous on planet Earth. We share this surprising attribute with one other extant life form on this planet, and this unavoidable correlation speaks volumes, both for the artificiality of our genesis, as well as for the probable reason for our race being brought into existence.

On Earth there is a race of beings who owe their existence to the human race. This race also produces the occasional 'genius' of its own. As a race it is equally anomalous in terms of Darwinian evolutionary theory as we ourselves are, and probably for the self-same reason: that natural selection did not produce it in its present form. Indeed, it could not have produced it in its present form, because it was called into being to serve purposes far removed from the mere necessities of survival of the fittest. However, although it was bred to serve purposes more 'advanced' than those served 'naturally' by its wild cousins, it was not produced to achieve eventual parity with its creators. Therefore, in all probability, neither were we.

Taking the foregoing as an indication of where the truth might be, and if, as I suspect, evolutionary theory has very little to do with humankind's real genesis, perhaps it is not out of bounds to look towards the Biblical account of our creation in our search for our roots. There is no doubt that the Bible, in particular Genesis, is a copy of a much more ancient version of what was possibly, a purely verbal tradition to begin with. That Genesis is a garbled account of something real is argued by the fact that the original on which it drew had two separate creation stories. However, in pursuit of their own monodeific propaganda:

> The scribes who attempted to put together the encyclopedia of history we call The Bible made some progress in their own way and according to their own understanding. The result is a religion now flourishing in this world and maintaining that there was only one Cycle of Creation, when anybody capable of reading the first chapters of its Holy Book, in any good translation, quite literally falls over two.[25]

By carefully separating the two accounts, it can be surmised that the first creation story dealt, quite scientifically within the parameters of the language used, with Univeral beginnings. The second addressed itself to events that occurred exclusively on this planet. Shorn of its allegedly religious ramifications, it seems to me that Genesis is trying to tell us that at some point in the remote past our race was called into being to serve specific purposes on behalf of individuals who had no particular aversion to being thought of as gods; perhaps, compared to their creature – us – they were. Without falling into the trap of anthropocentric speculation, the best that can be said about Genesis is that it is probably the remains of a factual account of a significant event that has been misunderstood and misinterpreted because the story was transmitted to posterity via people who eventually forgot what it was they were recounting. Fortunately (or unfortunately depending on your viewpoint), we still have ourselves from which to draw inspiration, and by this means answer our original question of how humankind became so variegated. The clue is supplied by that other variegated race, referred to earlier:

> Think of the enormous variety of breeds of dogs, from the Pekinese to the Great Dane, so entirely different from one another that a Martian might deny that they could be of the same species. And how did the dog species become so variegated – *only by manipulated breeding.*[26]

It has to be assumed that the same applies to us, because this would resolve all anomalies left untouched by evolutionary theory, while at the same time making it unnecessary to invoke some 'supernatural', Universe-creating deity to explain our existence on earth. It is this affinity that we, as a species, have with dogs that argues most strongly against evolution and for creation – of a sort – when trying to discover human origins. And which explains the real reason for the existence of the female hymen: the value in terms of breeding strategy is obvious.

Taking Genesis at face value, it seems to be saying that we were bred by a non-human life form as a kind of pet. That breeding did take place is shown by the fact that, like the dogs we have bred, there is an unnatural variegation in our species. Nature is not so demanding, and is seemingly satisfied with minimal differentiation between individuals, even between the sexes, within any given species. Apparently, only intelligently directed breeding can produce differentiation within species on the scale of that seen in dogs . . . or humankind. As further proof that, although probably bred from some wild life form, we have no relationship with monkeys, it can be pointed out that dogs can still mate with the other wild descendants (i.e., wolves) of their joint ancestor and produce viable offspring. Physical differences aside, their doggy chromosomes match. From this it should therefore be logical to assume that we should be able to mate with the descendants (i.e., gorillas *et al.*) of the wild stock from which we both allegedly stem, and produce viable offspring. Of course, we cannot do this because our chromosomes do not match. This alone is strongly indicative of too much monkey business when it comes to evolutionary allegations about our anthropoidal ancestry.

References

[1] 'Missing Presumed Non-Existent', Norman C. Wood, UFO Debate, Vol. 3, No. 5, Oct. 1992.

[2] ibid.

[3] Origins, Robert Shapiro (Penguin, 1988).

[4] Wood, op. cit.

[5] The Hot-blooded Dinosaurs, Adrian J. Desmond (Futura, 1977).

[6] Evolution, C. Patterson (Routledge & Keegan Paul, 1978).

[7] Mankind, Child of the Stars, Max Flint and Otto Binder (Fawcett Publications, 1974).

[8] The Descent of Man, Charles Darwin (Hurst & Co.).

[9] 'A Funny Thing Happened (on the way to extinction)', C. A. O'Conner, UFO Debate, Vol. 2, No. 5, Oct. 1991.

[10] Flint and Binder, op. cit.

[11] In Search Of Ancient Mysteries, A. and S. Landsburg (Corgi Books, 1974).

[12] Mysteries Of Time & Space, Brad Steiger (Prentice Hall, 1974).

[13] ibid.

[14] Worlds Before Our Own, Brad Steiger (W. H. Allen, 1980).

[15] ibid.

[16] ibid.

[17] Before Civilisation, Colin Renfrew (Knopf, 1973).

[18] Flint and Binder, op. cit.

[19] Darwin Retried, Norman MacBeth (Gambit Inc, 1971).

[20] 'Editor's Introduction', J. W. Burrow in Origin of the Species, Charles Darwin (Penguin, 1968).

[21] O' Connor, op. cit.

[22] Flint and Binder, op. cit.

[23] Our Ancestors Came From Outer Space, Maurice Chatelain (Dell, 1979).

[24] Flint and Binder, op. cit.

[25] The Sky People, Brinsley le Poer Trench (Neville Spearman, 1960).

[26] Flint and Binder, op. cit.

CHAPTER 2
Apocalypse BC

DURING the early part of this century it was fashionable for school children to be taught that the atom was indivisible, that faster than sound travel was impossible, that computers would never be much use because of the size of their vacuum tubes, and that the dinosaurs were a failed phylum that nature had dispensed with in favour of wonderful us. The first three (and many other similar scientific superstitions from the past) have been proven spectacularly wrong. The fourth will almost certainly be proved to be as false as the others. Up until very recently it was the Victorian view of dinosaurs that predominated. When portrayed, they were shown as lumbering leviathans whose sole purpose in life was to eat or be eaten. All kinds of attributes – in the main, unlikely, but flattering to the human ego – were ascribed to them by Victorian scientists from the fossil material being discovered. It was all so exciting that it did not seem to occur to anybody that if the evolutionary theory, just then coming into fashion, had any validity, then the dinosaurs, far from being an evolutionary failure could well have been its finest flowering. For, logically, if 'survival of the fittest' could produce the likes of us from mammalian stock in well under 70 million years, then, almost certainly, it would have done even better with the dinosaurs, who apparently flourished for 150 million years. This is a major flaw in mindless mechanistic processes, assuming they exist: they act impartially on everything to produce inevitable results.

Is it possible that there ever was an intelligent dinosaur? Or, put another way, is it possible that evolution, as envisioned by Darwin, could fail to produce an intelligent dinosaur? From what is now known of them, it seems unlikely. The difficulty is in getting palaeontologists to admit that their interpretation of the fossil record is faulty and illogically biased in favour of our cultural anthropomorphisms that won't let us see ourselves as anything other than the pinnacle of the evolutionary process. Modern palaeontologists seem not to be averse to spotting the

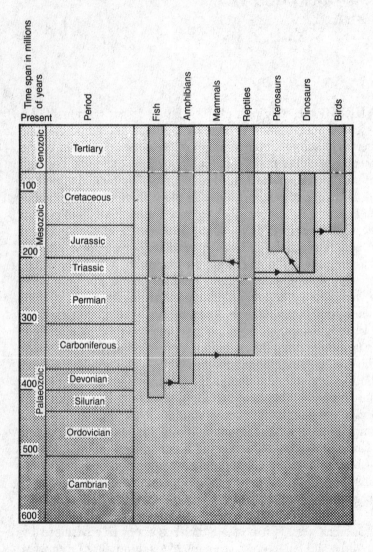

Figure 1 *Bar chart detailing history of vertebrate evolution according to mainstream palaeontology.*

mote in the eye of their scientific predecessors by readily admitting that: 'In the early 1900s palaeontologists often set up new dinosaur species on the evidence of scanty material, sometimes as little as a single vertebra or tooth.'[1]

However, they are quite blind to the beam in their own eye which enables them to produce charts (see Figure 1) detailing the progress of life on Earth which have glaring, and illogical, inconsistencies. Presumably these have been brought about by their ongoing efforts to avoid admitting anything that might indicate creation rather than blind chance had some influence on the appearance and continuation of life on Earth, especially human life. Figure 1 is based on diagram in *The Hot-blooded Dinosaurs* by A.J. Desmond. In the book, Desmond argues convincingly that the dinosaurs were warm blooded like ourselves, and not the cold-blooded reptilians they were always popularly thought to be. That they could have been something else is demonstrated in Figure 2, which shows a more plausible, more logical, progression of life on this planet. From this it can be clearly seen that, unlike the evolutionary anarchy portrayed in Figure 1, each phylum had just one evolutionary offshoot that then became the next dominant. Because of this demonstrably logical progression in life on Earth, and the fact that mammals apparently appeared on the scene at almost the same time as the dinosaurs, it is possible to surmise that the dinosaurs were just a superior type of mammal; that, in fact, the classification 'Dinosaur', is possibly just another example of that Victorian ineptitude whereby 'remains of animals of what we now know to be the same species were often given different names'.[2] Indeed, from the data in Desmond's book, it is possible to deduce that if dinosaurs had borne live young, instead of laying eggs, the two evolutionary developments of 'Dinosaur' and 'Mammal' would have been indistinguishable. It is possible from the case of the duck-billed platypus to argue that egg laying is no guarantee of non-mammalian classification. According to popular palaeontology, one of the evolutionary 'advances' of mammals was to 'live bear' their young instead of laying eggs. The One White Crow of that particular philosophy is none other than 'the Duck Billed Platypus. A contradiction in terms if ever there was one. Why? Because the creature is an egg-laying mammal – or so we are told.'[3] But what if it is really a dinosaur? What if the present

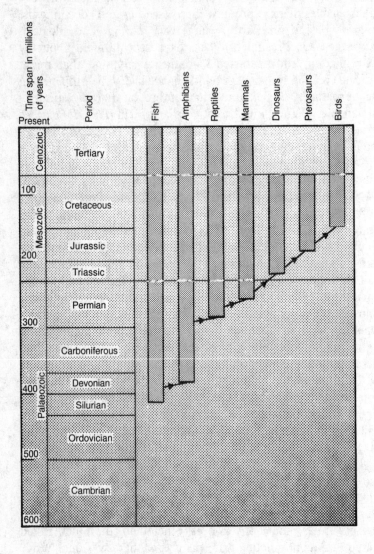

Figure 2 *History of vertebrate evolution rationalized according to the evolutionary alternative of atheistic creationism.*

distinction between dinosaurs and mammals is a false one? This can be suspected from the rationalized data in the Figure 2 which indicates that the development of warm-blooded creatures was a singular event; just as we now have in the antipodean duck-billed platypus an 'egg-laying mammal', there could equally well have been 'live-bearing dinosaurs'. Or more logically just one warm-blooded evolutionary development that produced creatures which have, due to the ignorance or whatever of our scientific ancestors, been misidentified into two different species. Perhaps we should not judge them too harshly in that a cataclysm – the possible causes of which generate much palaeontological head scratching – threw a spanner into the evolutionary works by nearly ending life on Earth for good and all. The question must now be: Was that an evolutionary accident, a natural occurrence, an act of God in the Biblical sense – or something else?

At this point, we can return to the statement by Oswaldo Reig: 'Disregarding the peculiar phenomenon of human evolution, we have to agree that the triumph of the Dinosaurs and their relations has been the major accomplishment in land vertebrate evolution.'[4] To answer the question about why humankind must be considered a 'peculiar development': there is nothing in the present evolutionary theory to account for us, although ongoing attempts are always being made to compel evolutionary theory to take account of our existence. In some ways our existence seems more explicable in terms of 'the major accomplishment in land vertebrate evolution' – the dinosaurs, which, in one form or another, filled every ecological niche on the planet; so why not also that of an intelligent life form? Is it only an unadmitted emotional predisposition to anthropocentricism that makes us reluctant to answer in the affirmative?

For 150 million years the dinosaurs ruled a world that was seemingly stable. During that almost incomprehensible length of time, they proliferated and diversified. Eventually,

They took over all the large roles in the land ecosystem. They filled the offices of mega-predator and mega-herbivore. Their control of the land ecosystem was complete. No nondinosaur larger than a modern turkey walked the land during the Age of Dinosaurs.[5]

Unarguably, the dinosaurs produced types to fill every ecological niche available . . . with one notable exception. It seems almost inconceivable that a dynamic species like the dinosaurs never produced a being to fulfil our role in a world they obviously ruled from first to last, especially in view of the fact that 'dinosaurs evolved quickly, changed repeatedly, and turned out wave after wave of new species with new adaptations all through their long reign'.[6] But what if, in fact, dinosaurs did produce an intelligent being? They certainly had all the right equipment for it. Above all, they had the necessary amount of geological time at their disposal for a mechanistic 'survival of the fittest' evolution process to produce a 'big brain'.

Furthermore, the two physical attributes most touted as the reasons for humankind's rise to intelligence are abundant among the dinosaurs. Firstly, the truly opposable thumb – while nowhere to be found in anthropoid development – has been demonstrated to have been prevalent among dinosaurs, in particular, in a creature called a Hypsilophodon, which has been described as a probable tree-dweller, very much like a monkey. Secondly, that other physical characteristic, a permanently upright stance which frees the hands with their opposable thumbs for 'tool using', is a strong dinosaur trait. Apparently, at least five types of dinosaur, including the Hypsilophodon, had this permanently upright stance. Thus, it can be argued that the evolutionary prerequisites for developing intelligence were to be found in abundance among the dinosaurs. It is therefore more probable that we had our genesis during the age of the dinosaurs, even if we merely 'evolved'; and if we were 'made' it is more probable that – with our anomalous physiognomy previously described – we were more likely 'bred' by intelligent dinosaurs from wild stock running about in their own age, but now extinct. In fact, whichever way you look at it, it seems more logical and likely that we are products of the Age of Dinosaurs and not the Age of Mammals, which possibly accounts for our easy dominance of the mammalian world in which we find ourselves. This is quite understandable if our racial beginnings were part of a development which is admitted to have been 'the major accomplishment in land vertebrate evolution', and which, once it got its start, swept away:

the last remnants of very advanced and very specialized clans, zoological tribes which had been evolving and perfecting their adaptive equipment for tens of millions of years,[7]

and then went on to become the undisputed masters of planet Earth, and

kept their commanding position for an extraordinary span of time.[8]

These facts make even more inexplicable their sudden disappearance *en masse* at a time that we now know was the dinosaurs' doomsday.

For reasons still somewhat unclear, some 70 million years ago the whole of the dinosaur world disappeared: 'Whatever the nature of the event we are dealing with it was of cataclysmic proportions.'[9] It was Apocalypse BC, and if, as this work attempts to argue, humankind was around at the time, then it is likely that Armageddon came and went 70 million years ago, and that those who now see visions and prophesy doom and disaster in the future are, in all probability, drawing on the racial memories of that global holocaust. Whatever the cause of the death of the dinosaurs:

The magnitude of the devastation cannot be overestimated. While the obliteration of all large and medium sized animals, coupled with the disruption of marine life, profoundly altered the direction that Life On Earth was to take.[10]

This disaster, which ended the dinosaurs' long reign on Earth, is admitted by palaeontology to have been a 'geologically sudden' event. Exactly how 'sudden' is still a matter for debate, but estimates have ranged from 'less than one million years', and 'tens of thousands of years', to 'a matter of a few days'. Despite this, it is accepted that at the close of the Cretaceous period, the Earth's ecosystem collapsed in a calamity of global proportions. Even so, there are those who still feel that the extinction of the dinosaurs was not unique in prehistory but that it can be easily explained away as just another extinction along the lines of those that occurred at the end of the Permian, Triassic and Jurassic periods: 'Altogether the stratigraphic record indicates eight sudden mass extinctions among the dominant families, of large, land dwelling vertebrates.'[11] A persuasive enough hypothesis, except that the wipe-out at the end of the Cretaceous period exceeded in magnitude all the other extinctions in that it did not just get rid of the dominant families of dinosaurs (i.e., T. Rex, Triceratops, Parasaurolophus, etc.), it got rid of the lot. The entire planet, land and sea, flora and fauna, apparently went into an almost terminal decline. However, even if the initiating event was 'geologically sudden', and no doubt removed a good portion of those then living, the real killer of the dinosaurs was the lingering after-effects which extended the terminal power of the catastrophe into geological time. Some of these after-effects were so similar to what is caused by residual radiation that palaeontology invoked 'nearby supernova' as an explanation. Yet this left another after-effect quite unaccounted for. It was equally as lethal, and this time attested to by the fossil record. This, in conjunction with the anomalously high radiation levels, was an anomalously large amount of dust present in the atmosphere. It was sufficient to cause a considerable drop in global temperatures; a drop so severe that creatures and plants used to living in Eden-like subtropical conditions withered away. To account for its presence, palaeontology once again invoked 'cosmic-coincidence' by adding a hypothetical asteroid strike to the equally hypothetical nearby supernova. Really, it would have taken the ingenuity of God to make these two hypothetical events coincide in time and space to affect the Earth simultaneously. Due to the restrictions imposed by the speed of light, the supernova, no matter how 'near by' in galactic terms, would have had to explode at a very precise moment, the correct number of years before the asteroid struck the Earth, to make the two events simultaneous from Earth's point of view. As you can appreciate, all solutions so far enumerated seem to leave begging the question of what exactly did kill the dinosaurs?

Only one event can properly explain their extinction, while at the same time combining in that explanation the aspects of 'sudden event' and 'lingering lethal after-effects' which seem to strain palaeontology's ability to come up with an answer. In suggesting another, less cosmically coincidental, explanation, palaeontology compares the conditions at the end of the Cretaceous period to a nuclear winter with 'radiation levels like those following a Nuclear War, global storms of extreme intensity, and disastrously low temperatures'.[12] So, if it really was nuclear war, who dropped the Bomb? The intelligent dinosaurs? Or, as the Bible seems to imply, were we in some way mixed up in it . . . the proto-human race just doing business as usual?

I know I would have difficulty in getting present-day palaeotologists to consider the idea that humankind is a lethal leftover from something that started during the Age of the Dinosaurs. Even if they could bring themselves to acknowledge the existence of all his various contra-mammalian attributes, they would still experience difficulty in seeing past the demands of their scientific belief system. The probability that humankind is a living fossil is a difficult point to make, but unless you are content to give God a bad name by accusing Him of being our creator 4004 years ago, there must be another alternative to explain why we are the way we are. Even if we are not dinosaurs in the classic sense, it seems we are so radically different from mammals – in fact to all life presently extant – that the likelihood of our having evolved from some unfound and ill-defined 'common ancestor' with gorillas and chimps is minuscule. But could the dinosaurs have produced a really intelligent being? One far more intelligent than us, and with talents we would consider paraphysical (i.e., supernatural, psychic, etc.), which then bred us from some wild dinosaur form as a kind of dinosaur dog? Given our anomalous physical attributes, and our strange and anomalous variations within the species, the answer must surely be . . . probably.

It is known that dinosaurs had among their number candidates for intelligence that evolution could have used to bring forth the dinosaur equivalent of us . . . or better. In fact, it has been palaeontologically speculated, 'If dinosaurs were warm blooded as far back as the Triassic, it could be expected that at least one of their later lines might have evolved some sort of higher intelligence.'[13] Apparently some did: the velociraptor, according to Spielberg in *Jurassic Park*. But that was fiction. In reality there was the Stenonychosaurus, whose fossil remains were found in the Judith River sediments in Alberta. It probably wasn't the only contestant. From what we now know of the dinosaurs, it is quite clear that either they were quick or they were dead – a valuable spur to evolution through natural selection. Palaeontologist Dale A. Russell, was intrigued enough by the possibility of an intelligent dinosaur that he imaginatively 'evolved' the Stenonychosaurus:

> By extrapolating its evolution until its ratio of brain weight to body weight was comparable to Homo Sapiens, the researcher came up with, and constructed a model of, a so-called dinosauroid.[14]

It was all hypothetical, of course, and allegedly could not have happened in reality because:

> Unfortunately the larger brained dinosaurs were among the last, and the merciless hand of extinction fell upon them just as it fell on all the Late Cretaceous groups.[15]

I for one don't believe it. That comment is just another example of human chauvinism in action. Surely, if there is such a thing as natural evolution it is illogical for its proponents to insist, without reference to the least shred of real proof, that it produced human intelligence in well under 70 million years, while irrationally denying it the obvious possibility of doing the same for the dinosaurs, which were around for 150 million years. Even so, scientific objections to the evolution of an intelligent dinosaur would carry the day, except for one salient fact: the product of dinosaur evolution, that is a living being looking exactly like the one hypothesized by Russell, has been reportedly seen by large numbers of individuals the world over.

The creatures in question are called 'the greys' and they are closely connected with ufological abductions. From artists' impressions drawn from the descriptions given by a number of abductee/witnesses, they can be seen to be exactly like the being hypothesized by Russell. This being can be described as a 'biped with bulging forehead, scaly skin, and clawed hands capable of cleverly manipulating objects'.[16] However, the amazing similarity between the imagined intelligent dinosaur, and the entities described by UFO abductees only becomes heart-stoppingly apparent when illustrations of the two are brought together and compared. Independently, Russell's model dinosauroid and the drawings of 'the greys' both show a bipedal creature with newt-like skin, domed head, large eyes, clawed hands, and with features that included slits for nostrils and mouth, and no visible ears. The synchronicity of a bona fide scientist producing a visual facsimile of a being well known in UFO circles, is one that would have made Jung's day. It can only be presumed that the coincidence is valid because, from the comparison between illustrations based on abductee testimony and Russell's model, it can be seen that the UFO witnesses and the hypothesizing palaeontologist are talking about the same being, and presumably without either of them being aware of the curious convergence of their descriptions. Can the UFO-related creatures be the intelligent dinosaur survivors of the nuclear accident, or deliberate war, that so enervated the Earth at the close of the Cretaceous? Perhaps, you may concede, but what has that to do with us? Is it or is it not a fact that we were not around at that time when these creatures met their evolutionary Waterloo, because according to the gospel of palaeontology, 'Fortunately or unfortunately, however, more than sixty million years separate the last dinosaur from the first human being.'[17] But what if palaeontology is wrong? What if we, along with the UFO entities, are living leftovers from the Age of the Dinosaurs – or before? Well, there are indications that man and dinosaur met in the prehistoric past, but what their exact relationship was is unclear from the scanty fossil evidence. Fossil evidence that, yet again, mainstream palaeontology seems determined to ignore.

There seems little doubt that the strongest evidence for humankind and the dinosaurs being contemporaneous comes in the form of fossil footprints. Already mentioned are the ones found in 1968 in Utah, among which was one that Dr Clifford Burdick, a consulting geologist, unambiguously claimed was 'exactly what it appears to be – the barefoot print of a child'.[18] And what of the ones mentioned by Henry Schoolcraft as being found in a crinoidal limestone slab on the west bank of the Mississippi River at St Louis, Missouri? According to him, they gave every evidence of having been left by a man standing erect in a natural position. They were 'strikingly natural, exhibiting every muscular impression, and the swell of heel and toes.'[19] Perhaps the most incredible aspect of these 'fossil footprints' is not that they are there, but that they obviously belonged to a life form that resembled modern man, at least as far as its feet were concerned. Well, just like Robinson Crusoe, I know what footprints in the sand mean . . . even in the sands of time. Of course, it isn't so easy for palaeontologists to admit that their carefully constructed cosmologies might be wrong. With all the fervour of Bible Belt Fundamentalists, they perform feats of intellectual legerdemain to avoid accepting the kind of evidence that would seem to indicate a lifespan for humankind well out of the range of that proposed by present-day evolutionary theory. Like the ufological 'debunkers', they seem capable of countenancing any outré explanation so long as it leaves their evolutionary edifice intact; but the situation is not helped by claims of bona fide fossil dinosaur prints being found in the same beds as fossil human prints, for this would inevitably mean that 'scientists will be forced either to place man back in time to the Cretaceous period or to bring the dinosaurs forward'.[20] Either way, unacceptable as the idea might be to Establishment palaeontology, it would mean that humankind and the dinosaurs had an as yet palaeontologically unadmitted interface in time. And the conclusions to be drawn from that is what this book is all about.

It is time now to return to our theme of human beings as a specifically bred life form. It is possible that, if this is anywhere near the truth, we will stand in relation to our breeders in exactly the same way as dogs stand to us. Those who bred us would have had powers and abilities that would have made them forever superior to their creation, but also that that creation – us – would have had resources unavailable to our creators, which would have made us a very dangerous pet indeed. We are, I like to think, the Pit Bulls of dinosaur pet breeding, and I think the content of Genesis proves that beyond a doubt. Before discussing the Genesis material, let us try to ascertain from what natural species our wild forebears came before the dinosaur breeding techniques modified us into what we finally became. We must have started life as a reptile derivative of some kind. Reptiles, of course, were the life form immediately preceding the dinosaurs, and out of which they and mammals evolved. Somehow this allegedly cold-blooded creature produced the warm-blooded development that not only led to mammals and dinosaurs, but also to birds. Clearly, something is presently wrong with the palaeontological position in these matters; but at the moment it is our concern to indicate where humankind came from, and not to take issue with the entire body of palaeontological knowledge to date, no matter how shaky its foundations appear to be. As there is, even today, a mix of creatures living (i.e., reptiles, marsupials, mammals), it can be confidently assumed it was the same in the geological past, and that our real ancestor – some kind of warm-blooded reptile – was living in a world rapidly being taken over by the dinosaurs, That we have evolutionary credentials going back far in geological time is possible by the fact that 'very primitive reptiles of all kinds had collarbones (clavicles) that braced the shoulder blades (humans retain this primitive bony strut, as do most lizards)'.[21] If, as has been demonstrated in the preceding chapter, we are not mammals, which supposition the above quote seems to support, then it must mean that in the search for our beginnings we are not limited to the meagre 70 million years that comprise the Age of Mammals.

If the analogy is accurate, then the dog/human relationship would parallel as near as makes no difference the probable ongoing, and growing, relationship between the intelligent dinosaurs and our ancestors. The result would be almost identical with the one we imposed upon dogs in that we became 'domesticated' and flourished, while others of our kind were forced into extinction as the dinosaur varieties took over the world. Then something went wrong, and we apparently became the enemy of those who bred us. As this remove in time, it is impossible to be sure exactly what happened. Folklore, legend, and religious myth all point to there being some kind of cosmic confrontation (i.e., Ragnarok, the War in Heaven) for which we – for reasons still unclear – apparently must take most of the blame. It must have been a major encounter, because it seems to have left its mark throughout the solar system in the form of craters on the various planets, and an asteroid belt where once a planet probably orbited. Of course, when dealing with the remote past, the trouble is that no matter from what body of 'evidence' you draw your inspiration, you are, in effect, whistling in the dark. During the time periods involved, almost anything could have happened and left no real footprints in the sands of geological time. From the Eden-like myth in Genesis it is possible to infer that, after 'the war in heaven' (whatever that concept was originally intended to convey), we were demoted from favoured pet to some kind of working watchdog, caretaker/gardener, status. Exactly how long this state of affairs lasted is difficult to guess; but then, we somehow put our foot in it . . . again? It is recorded in Genesis in such form that it is difficult to interpret; yet there it is. It is clear from the account that the being alleged to be God probably wasn't. His behaviour, as recorded in the Genesis account, is more akin to that of earthly dictators who are well aware of their own vulnerability, or perhaps of bureaucrats who know they have let something happen that reveals them as something less than omnipotent. If taken at face value – and this is one of the strongest indications that Genesis is more than just a pioous fable – the Eden 'myth' clearly shows that, far from being an omnipotent Universal Creator, the individual who confronted the de-programmed Adam and Eve was a fallible individual whose attempt to 'domesticate' humankind had gone disastrously wrong. Considering our reptilian credentials, it seems synchronous, to say the least, that a 'serpent' was the alleged *agent provocateur* in this 'fall from grace'. In respect of our 'keeper' – the God who never was – perhaps he was just a manager, or a civil servant of sorts, but it is made quite clear in Genesis that the fact that Adam and Eve had 'eaten of the fruit of the tree of the knowledge of Good and Evil' fairly put the wind up him. Also, this same account proves that he wasn't some monotheistic deity, because he tells his peers that Adam and Eve had become one of them, and that our 'first parents' had to be thrown out of Eden before they had the chance to eat from the Tree of Life and so become immortal. In all probability, in Genesis, we are dealing with a mythologized account of a very real happening which does not refer to individuals but to a clash between races, of which ours was the alleged inferior, or underdog. Whatever really happened, it was probably the trigger for the nuclear war that closed the Cretaceous period and very nearly did for both us and our dinosaur breeders. There is very little doubt, from the dialogue in Genesis, that 'God' was quite terrified of our first parents, and regarded them as monsters of Frankenstinian proportions – hence all the threats and ill temper. I know that religionists have a habit of insisting that the Bible is relevant to today's world. I agree that it probably is – but not quite in the way that they mean. If the Genesis account does relate in some way to real events at the end of the Cretaceous period, then it has taken both us and the dinosaurs a long time to recover from the results of that confrontation. We now have really become like one of 'them', wielding god-like powers, while our growing medical and biological expertise gets us ready to take a bite at the apple of immortality. If 'they' are still around, as the 'abduction experience' indicates, then I wonder what 'they' will do about that this time?

It now seems almost inevitable that the world cannot keep going in the way it is presently doing without coming to grief. An end of some description is very nigh, and try as we might we cannot discipline ourselves to avoid it. Almost perceptibly, week by week, we grow less and less 'domesticated' as we apparently 'devolve' back to what we were before. The veneer of civilization is falling from us in just the same way that dogs, without the continuing supervision of their masters, will form themselves into packs and revert to more 'natural' behaviour patterns. In other words, like the dogs we bred from the wild, without the supervision of those who bred us, we have a strong tendency to revert to the wild. Such devolutionary behaviour is dangerous enough in dogs, but in our case it could be terminal for all concerned. In some strange way, we seem to know it, and yearn for the return of our masters – the *deus ex machina* delusion that underpins the unrealistic hopes of those who too easily believe that the 'Spacebrothers' will save them . . . this time from Apocalypse AD?

References

[1] *The Reign of the Dinosaurs*, Jean-Guy Michard (Thames & Hudson, 1982).

[2] ibid.

[3] ' A Funny Thing Happened (on the way to extinction)', C. A. O'Conner, *UFO Debate*, Vol. 2, No. 5, Oct. 1991.

[4] ibid.

[5] *The Dinosaur Heresies*, Robert Bakker (Penguin, 1980).

[6] ibid.

[7] ibid.

[8] ibid.

[9] *The Hot-blooded Dinosaurs*, Adrian J. Desmond (Futura, 1977).

[10] ibid.

[11] Bakker, op. cit.

[12] Desmond, op. cit.

[13] Bakker, op. cit.

[14] Michard, op. cit.

[15] Bakker, op. cit.

[16] ibid.

[17] Michard, op. cit.

[18] *Mysteries of Time & Space*, Brad Steiger (Prentice Hall, 1974).

[19] ibid.

[20] *Worlds Before Our Own*, Brad Steiger (W. H. Allen, 1980).

[21] Bakker, op. cit.

CHAPTER 3

Before Adam Was a Lad

THE PAST, especially the remote prehistoric past is something of a closed book, whatever the 'ologies' concerned in investigating and interpreting it might maintain. However, by accepting their information and assuming, just for the sake of argument, that we were 'bred' by an intelligent dinosaur race from wild stock that was similar in function, if not in kind, to the wild dogs that humankind later domesticated, it might be possible to deduce from extant palaeontological information if any fossil evidence supports the idea of our existence in days well before conventional scholarship would admit that Adam was a lad.

It really is strange how myths relating to a golden age that was destroyed in a global cataclysm seem persistently to permeate the folklore of races who, according to science, were not even aware of each other's existence. The biblical account of the 'Flood', for example, finds its echoes in far-away America, where any number of native American Indians cherish legends that 'tell of their people rising from the destruction that had been visited upon a former civilization'.[1] The Biblical account itself appears to be only an echo of a similar tale of which another, and probably older, version can be found in the Sumerian 'Epic of Gilgamesh'. Even so, the Genesis account clearly indicates that we were called into existence for almost the selfsame reason we bred dogs: to be a slave in perpetuity to the life form that bred us. That we 'rebelled' against such constraint, and thereby caused a commotion of some kind, is interesting information, however it is interpreted. Now, the question must be: could all the various 'catastrophe myths' endemic in our various cultures have as their template the one colossal cataclysm that ended the Eden experiment, and was that the cataclysm that almost ended everything at the close of the Cretaceous period?

Palaeontological purists will have none of the notion that we, as a race, date back to the dinosaurs, preferring the orthodox dogma of evolutionary science of which:

> The academic concensus holds that an ancestor of modern man evolved about one million years ago. Homo Sapiens, 'thinking man', our own species, became the dominant planetary life form on a worldwide basis about 40,000 years ago.[2]

However, it is demonstrable that such a scenario is a palaeontological fantasy. In reality, the picture is more confused. What evolutionary sense can be made of the find in Australia 'which yielded Homo Sapiens (modern man), Homo Erectus (our million-year-old ancestor?), and Neanderthal (our stone-age cousin?) in what appears to be a contemporaneous environment'?[3] This can only mean that they all were living at the same time, and in the same place – an impossibility if evolutionary theory were true. But things get immeasurably worse when you consider the content of the Tabun site 'where Homo Sapiens fragments were found in strata below (which means older than) classic Neanderthal bones'.[4] Tabun is not the only site where this anomalous placement of fossil bones has been found. Suitably confused? If you are, then you would never make a palaeontologist, and you had better not even think about the pre-Adamite fossil record, because most palaeontologists don't, which means that many questions about our real ancestry go begging.

The trouble with many of the pre-Adamite finds is that they indicate that, not only was humankind living at the time of the dinosaurs, he was possibly correspondingly large. One particular find at Glen Rose, Texas, of a 16-in (41-cm) hominid footprint next to dinosaur tracks in the same strata clearly indicates that man and monster lived at the same time. In confirmation of this, 'Skeletal remains of surprisingly large human beings have been discovered all over the Americas, from Minnesota to Nicaragua.'[5] Strange to tell, or perhaps not, the finds at Glen Rose, Texas, are mentioned in a bona fide palaeontological work, but somehow the tracks that accompanied the brontosaur tracks were transmuted into those of an unidentified 'flesh eater' even after the admission

that there were so many of these tracks that they had been dug out
and incorporated into local buildings:

> The town, it seems, had long taken such 'man tracks' for
> granted. They occurred in large numbers on the bed of the
> local Paluxy River some miles upstream where the river was
> cutting through Lower Cretaceous mudflats and exposing the
> footprints.[6]

These 'man tracks' are later turned into the tracks of an
unspecified 'flesh eater' without comment by the author,
nevertheless:

> There were other serious Glen Rose residents who testified as
> to genuine human footprints in the bed of the Paluxy River.
> One man told of finding a series of tracks in which what
> appeared to have been a leather thong on one moccasin flopped
> in the mud as its wearer strode about his business.[7]

From the sounds of it, the 'humans' were there hunting or
herding brontosaurs. Either way, the possibility that we were
there at all is staggering, and palaeontology is remiss in its
professional duty in not considering such strange fossil finds
seriously.

In attempting to clarify humankind's very early history, there
is much obfuscation to remove from the path. It is clear from the
fossil record (what there is of it) that something peculiarly like
modern man was wandering about the world before Adam was
allegedly a glint in the eye of the Almighty. Yet, much later in
time, that same fossil record shows that degenerate forms of
'hominids' were plentiful, while true man seemed to have gone
into eclipse, in fact:

> The evolution tree has many branches – often, in fact,
> resembling more a bramble thicket than a simple elm or ash –
> and from these twisting branches any number of discovered
> and undiscovered species may swing.[8]

All these convolutions in our family tree make very little sense in
terms of the requirements of a 'survival of the fittest' evolutionary
theory. However, what if some of these various types of so-called

'man' were the product of radiation-generated mutation, and in fact represented a 'devolution' of the original bipedal being bred by the dinosaurs. This scenario might even explain why, in this day and age, the human race is still susceptible to genetically transmitted diseases that produce infants fated never to achieve the full human potential. Can it be that 70 million years on we are still paying for our temerity, or foolhardiness, in defying those who bred us?

One of the difficulties in coming to terms with possible unpalatable truths from the past is that even today, with our sophisticated methods of dating fossil finds, there is still no real palaeontological consensus on what those fossil bones reveal: 'There are those scientists who would speak of all primates who occurred before Homo Sapiens, or at the outside, before Homo Erectus, as being apes, not men.'[9] Almost assuredly, there would be others who would propose almost the opposite. Such scholarly semantic contests sometimes have very little to do with these dry bones, but more to do with the defence of some professor's perceived place in the palaeontological pecking order. So, even though the difference between man and monkey is an important one to define, human nature being what it is, 'One man's man is another man's monkey, and the line of evolution is often knotted with semantic tangles.'[10] Even if we fall back on the material in the Genesis account, which in itself seems to be only an echo of earlier material (in particular the Sumerian 'Epic of Gilgamesh'), there seems to be no way to clarify the real origins of our species. But in studying the ancient sources with intuition at full blast, one cannot escape the feeling that despite the palaeontological view of the Age of Dinosaurs, if we were there – as the fossil 'erratics' tend to indicate we were – then the Mesozoic period, including as it does the Triassic, Jurassic and Cretaceous periods, must have been the nearest thing to paradise that we have ever experienced. Yet, it would seem, that despite this we 'rebelled', either against our dinosaur masters, or against the existing natural order, or both, in possibly the exact same fashion as we are doing today. Thus we brought about the destruction of the ecosystem, the death of the dinosaurs, and our own racial decline. Even now, it is possible that we have not fully recovered from this, because our race still seems susceptible to congenital diseases. As to the global cataclysm that closed the Cretaceous period with a bang, it is useless to speculate on the specifics, but the memory of those terrible times arguably influenced our global folklore forever after. This is possibly responsible for our feelings of racial guilt, as they apply to the concept of 'original sin'. So, as the dust (literally) began to settle on a wasting world, perhaps . . . 'we staggered into the future. Bereft of our senses, and wracked by radiation. While all around us grew the new dispensation.'[11] What the intelligent dinosaurs who bred us were doing at this time to save themselves will be the subject of a later chapter.

After the cataclysmic close of the Cretaceous period, our world must have been a wasteland. But time heals everything and in 70 million years a lot of healing can take place. The burgeoning mammals began to fill up the ecological niches left vacant by the dinosaurs. The vegetation recovered, but not in quite the same form. And among it all wandered what was left of the human race, its past forgotten, and its future uncertain. Untold ages rolled by while creatures who were not men, and never would be men appeared on, and disappeared from, the world stage. It is impossible from the findings of palaeontology, anthropology, and even archaeology, to connect these humanoid creatures to ourselves. Perhaps, as the fossil record allegedly indicates, they were related to each other in some way and they collectively represent a genuine evolutionary initiative to produce intelligence from the mammalian phylum. If so, its finest flowering would seem to have been Neanderthal man, who 'may have wandered, squatted about their fires in their caves, and died in Europe for a period extending over eighty thousand years'.[12] If that is true, then evolution passed them by because, from the evidence, it seems they altered not at all during the 80,000 years of their existence. It is entirely possible that these creatures were the last of the mammalian hominids, before the living fossil from the geological past came to reclaim his heritage. The creature in question was Cro-Magnon man, the true progenitor of ourselves, who appeared (re-appeared) on the scene somewhere between 20,000 and 30,000 years ago, and proceeded to take over the world. But where did he come from? There is no evidence to connect Cro-Magnon with any hominid that preceded him: he apparently appeared quite suddenly out of nowhere, equipped with brains slightly larger than ours, and – seemingly ignoring what was left of Neanderthal man – he began, as if working from memory, to create the basis for the world as we now know it. So sudden was the appearance of Cro-Magnon that some have speculated that he arrived from outer space, simply because evolutionary biology leans to the belief that nature does not make great leaps, or 'macromutations'. According to this evolutionary requirement, Cro-Magnon man should have taken a considerable amount of geological time to develop its 1590/1715 cc brains, and the skills it displayed on its arrival on the world stage. However, inexplicably for orthodox evolutionists – 'There is no evidence – either in skulls or artefacts – of this long transitionary period. The Cro-Magnons seem to have appeared with no warning.'[13]

As if they had dropped – fully pre-adapted for spaceflight, atomic manipulations and computer games – from a clear sky, Cro-Magnons set about the human adventure as to the manner born, which, of course, they probably were. Evolution appeared to come to a standstill when they (us in other words) arrived back on the sceen. Had we always been there, hidden by the radiation-generated mutations which dogged our path for nearly 70 Million years? The kind of natural evolution that produced us does not exist. All that remains is the semblance derived from an anthropomorphic reading of the fossil record by individuals who cannot countenance the idea that there might have existed beings intrinsically superior to us. What is needed to make that point is the kind of remains that would indicate the possibility of non-human constructors; the kind of ruins that just might have survived from the Cretaceous period. The amount of time involved is nothing short of collosal, and even if found, a construction's survival over such a lengthy period would be difficult to prove – but there are hints:

> At Baalbek, in modern Lebanon, the Romans constructed their magnificent temple to the sun, a temple which was dwarfed in size, however, by the immense prehistoric dressed-stone platform on which it was built. Of unknown age and origin, the platform is a feat of engineering that has never been equalled in history.[14]

The platform is made of stones weighing a staggering 1,500 tons each. These 80 ft by 15 ft by 15 ft (24 m by 5 m by 5 m) megaliths are laid with such precision that there would be difficulty in getting a knife blade between them. However, at the quarry where these gigantic stones were cut, there lies the daddy of them all, weighing in excess of 2,000 tons. Apparently abandoned by the original constructors, it still waits transportation to the others. Unfortunately, for the present possibilities of such an endeavour, 'There are no cranes or other lifting apparatus in the world today that can budge, let alone lift, the titanic blocks at Baalbek.'[15] Thus, the largest cut stone in the world (unless, of course *you* know better) must remain where it is until the original architects return to complete their work, and so clarify the puzzle of what it was they were building. Neither folklore nor science is able to explain adequately the mystery of the Baalbeck platform, but it appears that 'such blocks must have been put in place either by giants or by beings of a civilization that knew the secrets of levitation and anti-gravity'.[16] Similar to the statuary on Easter Island, some event stopped work on the platform before its completion. If the platform were the only extant example of possibly non-human architecture that could have survived from the truly prehistoric past, then cynical savants could be forgiven their scepticism of the possibility of civilizations superior to their own having existed in the remote past. But there is an equally mysterious example of cyclopean construction on the other side of the world – at Tiahuanaco in Peru.

Although it is generally accepted that the city of Tiahuanaco is pre-Inca in origin, this might mean very little, because it is also alleged that 'there are no authentic traditions about Tiahuanaco'.[17] This means that, as at Baalbek, nobody is quite sure who built it, or why, or when. There is even the suggestion that, as at Baalbek, it was abandoned before completion. Considering the site it occupies, 13,000 ft (3,960 m) above sea level, with an atmosphere so rarified that it can cause heart attacks, it is a wonder it was ever built at all. So you might think that such an undertaking would leave its mark in any extant mythology of the area. However, this does not seem to be the case; its origins are completely unknown, in fact, 'Not even the oldest living Indian could tell of its history when questioned by the Spanish Conquistadores in their bloody assault on the area in 1549.'[18] Well, that was very nearly 500 years ago, and although Tiahuanaco has been intensively studied since then, and several scientific suggestions regarding its origins and purpose have been put forward, no further conclusive clues to its originators have come to light. Hardly surprising, if it wasn't originally built where it now stands. There are clear signs in Tiahuanaco of a 'dockland', which suggests that, as a result of some planetary upheaval, the 'port' of Tiahuanaco 'was left stranded thousands of feet up the newly appeared Andes'.[19] However, the quarry which provides the stones to build Tiahuanaco has been located on an island in nearby Lake Titicaca. It is clear that this lake was once much larger, so Tiahuanaco would have been on its shores. The appellation 'seaport' seems a little extreme to explain docking facilities in the city. Despite this, it can be still maintained that cyclopean constructions, like Baalbek and Tiahuanaco, do argue strongly for a planetary pre-history far removed from the one presently propagated by the conventional palaeontological concensus.

As well as cyclopean ruins, of which Baalbeck and Tiahuanaco are only a representative sample, there is also evidence that points quite conclusively to nuclear war being a feature of prehistory. According to a story published in the *Herald Tribune* on 16 February 1947, archaeologists digging in the Euphrates valley found a layer of fused green glass beneath layers dating back in excess of 10,000 years. The disturbing thing about this find was that it resembled the layer of fused green glass that was found on the surface of the sand in the New Mexico desert at the site of the first atomic explosion:

> Lightning may occasionally fuse sand, but when it does, the fusing occurs in a distinctive, rootlike pattern. Could anything other than a nuclear explosion produce an entire layer, a whole stratum of fused green glass?[20]

Given the logic of similar causes producing similar effects, one would have to answer no, but that's not the end of it. Staying, for the present, in the United States, there is the problem of the vitrified remains of cities found in, the aptly named, Death Valley. A Captain Walker was the first to see one of the ruined cities, the centre piece of which was 'a huge rock, between 20 and 30 feet high, with the remains of an enormous structure atop it. The southern side of both the rock and the building was melted and vitrified.'[21] A follow-up expedition by a colleague of Captain Walker discovered even more, that in fact:

> The whole region between the rivers Gila and San Juan is covered with remains. The ruins of cities are to be found there which must be most extensive, and they are burnt out and vitrified in part, full of fused stones and craters caused by fires which were hot enough to liquefy rock or metal.[22]

At first, it was assumed that vulcanism was to blame for the vitrification. This seems unlikely as there are no volcanoes in the area – active or otherwise – and, in any case, tectonic heat is insufficiently intense to cause the kind of rock surface liquefaction displayed at sites like this one. Of course, there is more than one such site in this area: 'Other vitrified ruins have been found in parts of Southern California, Arizona and Colorado. The Mohave Desert is reported to contain several circular patches of fused glass.'[23] And when taken in conjunction with similarly vitrified remains which have been found in places as far apart as the north and south of India, Scotland, Norway, and even near to the ancient site of Babylon, this evidence is almost coincidentially conclusive of the contention of nuclear strikes in the past. But how far in the past? If we accept the conventional view – allegedly supported by fossil and archaeological finds – then humankind has never been able to produce a nuclear capability until now. So who dropped atom bombs in the Mohave Desert? And in India, Scotland and many other places, including South America? Just adjacent to the pre-Inca fortress of Sacsahuaman in Peru there is a huge area of fused and crystallized mountain rock. While in Brazil there are ruins known as Sete Ciddaes:

> The stones of these ruins have been melted by apocalyptic energies, and squashed between the layers of rock protrude bits of rusting metal that leave streaks like the traces of red tears down the crystallized wall surface.[24]

Clearly, something occurred in the past which orthodoxy seems unwilling to admit. But just because something contrary to Establishment scientific doctrine can't get admitted to the general consensus does not automatically mean it is incorrect: Galileo would vouch for that, I'm sure. So let us continue to pursue the allegedly outrageous just in case, metaphorically speaking, the world isn't quite as flat as present-day palaeontological pundits would have us believe.

For the moment, I will leave aside the almost conclusive evidence for nuclear technology in the remote past, even though – as readers are surely aware – the written traditions of India alone, with their tales of wars waged between deific beings utilizing weapons with names like 'Indra's dart' and the 'iron thunderbolt', more than confirm the past's nuclear capability, as well as the will to use it. Instead, I will turn to the most enduring mythology regarding vanished civilizations, indeed vanished continents and lost worlds. This concens Mu/Lemuria/Atlantis. The so-called 'legendary' material concerning these has probably been left to us by genetic memory – the collective unconscious of Jung – of the pre-Cretaceous civilizations of our dinosaur masters.

Almost certainly, the cataclysm which removed the dinosaurs was so traumatizing to our race that, even when it was long in the past, we used our confused memories of it as a source for con-structing mythologies of later disasters as we, in response to our genetic programming, sought to reconstruct past technologies. In effect, it is probable that all of humankind's mythological 'disaster stories' have at their root the cataclysm that closed the Cretaceous period, even though, over the millennia, our memories of those world-shaking events have inevitably become inextricably entangled with, and attributed to, lesser disasters that had more immediacy to present times. This is why the mythology regarding the 'sinking of Atlantis' can now be confidently attributed by scholars to the Thera eruption which ended the Minoan civilization, even though the original 'deluge' was more likely to have been just one of the after-effects of the Cretaceous ecocrash.

Although certain scholars might not like to think it, there is every chance that there once was, and still is, a place called Mu/Lemuria. It was identified by James Churchwarden as 'the motherland of man', and is probably planet Earth in its entirety, rather than any particular continent. At this remove in time, it is almost impossible to be precise about what happened on our planet in prehistory, but clues gleaned from a global folklore agree in principle about one major world changing event, and it is quite possible that at the core of these myths 'are in fact memories, half forgotten folk memories, of happenings in a long gone past'.[25] And if they are memories, what are they memories of? Something that deprived us of the very thing we were bred to serve, and in so doing laid the foundation of humankind's otherwise inexplicable religious impulse? Also, the seemingly inbred instinct to be subservient, the need to worship something 'greater' than ourselves? If humankind is, as evolutionists maintain, a natural product of Earth's ecosystem, of the mindless mechanics of evolution, from where came this seemingly inbred need for 'gods'? Can it be significant that the only other animal to display a need for similar submissiveness to its 'master' is the dog? In our quest for the truth about our race, unless we are willing to deduce from a plethora of strongly circumstantial evidence, we will inevitably remain in ignorance of what we are and why we behave the way we do. According to Immanuel Velikovsky, in an interview reported in *Science & Mechanics Magazine* in July 1968,

We have abundant references in literature – even in rabbinical literature – that many times . . . *before* this present Earth Age existed, in fact several times the *same* Earth was created – then it was levelled and recreated; all civilizations were buried. This was long, long *before* the time of the Biblical character, Adam.[26]

Nearly right, Immanuel, but in fact the ancient texts to which he refers, which describe geological disturbances of cataclysmic proportions, are garbled records of the events that ended the Cretaceous period and which occurred in times before modern science admits that 'Adam' (i.e., humankind) could have existed. But of course we did, otherwise how could Velikovsky conclude, in the best psychiatric tradition, that we seek to regain the trauma? Certainly, we seek to regain the terminal technology of the past, not because of some ill-defined amnesiac trauma, but because that was what we were probably bred for in the first place. To wax metaphorical, it is probable that we are the dinosaurs' dogs of war, their atomic android, bred to fight. Just look at world history, and I am sure you will get the picture.

Because of the momentousness of the event that became the ongoing 'template' against which all future local disasters were measured, it is almost certain that Mu/Lemuria/Atlantis were originally the same place, that they were not separate 'continents' or 'islands' or even 'civilizations' which sank beneath the sea. Originally, these names were applied to the entire Earth. That all ancient, mythological and unlocated places like 'the garden of Eden', Lemuria, and especially Mu, were originally references to the planet itself makes more understandable the garbled folklore about continents that allegedly plunged, aeons apart, beneath the waves. There was only one cataclysm of such magnitude, and that was at the end of the Cretaceous period. Life on Earth could not have survived a regular repetition of such global mayhem; it very nearly perished the first time. The experience was so upsetting that our entire race has been having cultural night-mares ever since. It might yet turn out to be the subconscious source of many of our inexplicable fears and phobias, both racial and individual.

Conventional science politely scoffs at the persistent efforts of those who accept the existence of Mu/Lemuria/Atlantis as fact and try to locate the original site. Science itself has 'located' Atlantis all over the place, but it mainly leans to the proposition that the Atlantis mythology grew out of a mish-mash of folklore dealing with purely local disasters. But, of course, science also subscribes to the idea that our ancestors were given to exaggeration and prone to attribute cosmic significance to events having a purely local impact. If at the base of all the disaster legends is the global tragedy of the Cretaceous period, then the 'location' of Mu/Lemuria/Atlantis will never be 'found' because it is the entire planet. The best that can ever be done is to locate the sites of subsequent local inundations to which the original mythos has been erroneously attributed in the folktales of the particular group of humans who experienced it. It is just too much of a coincidence that mysterious continents, with their locations in both the middle of the Pacific (Mu/Lemuria) and the middle of the Atlantic (Atlantis), both should have perished in the same way for the same reason. Almost certainly, when seeking an ancient civilization whose 'wicked' activities convulsed the world, there is only one place to look – the close of the Cretaceous period and the global event that caused an almost classic nuclear-winter scenario. Mu/Lemuria/Atlantis are the same civilization, in the same way as Libya, America, Russia, or if you prefer Europe,

North America and Australia are all the same global, 'Western' civilization today. Rather than searching for a 'lost continent', the existence of which science is probably right in ascribing to:

> philosophical parables told by Plato in order to provide a dramatic object lesson in civics for his students[27]

we must address relevant material in the realization that it is dealing with the end of a global civilization so far back in time that it is less than a memory of a memory we would like to forget. Then, we will probably find – yet again – that we and the dinosaurs had some kind of unsuspected interface over 70 million years ago.

Although superficially coherent, the mythology concerning the demise of Lemuria and Atlantis is unspecific, and far too general to be considered a reliable account of the underlying events which generated the mythos. A lot of the material reads like an apologia, by which I mean that a 'reasonable' explanation was attempted for what, in effect, was a totally unreasonable event. The explanatory difficulties are compounded by the various myth-makers confusing (deliberately or otherwise) earlier material with those which referred specifically to the event they were trying to make mythological capital out of. A good example of this process is how the delusions of grandeur of a small group of local people in the Middle East made them manipulate an already pre-existing (Mesozoic?) mythology to get 'God' on their side. Of course, once it is realized where this strange desire to have a 'special relationship' with a 'superbeing' comes from, much of history becomes that more understandable – especially when it is realized that the Jews are not the only people cherishing the 'chosen by god' syndrome. Ridiculously, we all seem prone to thinking that the imagined Universal Creator subscribes to our particular parochial belief system. It is probably just another indication of our genetic and racial conditioning that we do, because such 'beliefs' are demonstrably not natural. However, unnatural as they are, such aspirations were seemingly part of our psychological make-up from the start. It can only be seen as synchronous that the platform at Baalbek was used to raise yet another temple dedicated to an imagined deity, when it is realized that the word 'Baalbek' incorporates the name of the 'serpent deity', Baal.

Further evidence of our real connections to the 'superbeings' of the Cretaceous period are the ruins at Tiahuanaco, where our forebears 'worshipped' a 'Father of all Things' called Mut, who was personified by an egg. Dinosaurs laid eggs, and Mu, supposedly pronounced Moo, could easily have been spelled Mut, the 't' being silent. Also, it would seem that the highest-ranking deity was called 'the supreme armour-clad ruler'. Once again, it can be pointed out that even in present-day palaeontology any number of dinosaurs are referred to as being 'armour-clad'. Interestingly, the Caananites, who apparently had close ties with the 'god' Baal, 'never felt certain that winter would be followed by spring'.[16] For most of the dinosaurs caught in the catastrophe at the end of the Cretaceous summer, it never did. Yet if a modern mystery is anything to go by, some of them survived to the present time. It seems to me that the clues are all there. Perhaps those who originally interpreted them have erred in favour of the anthropomorphically grandiose.

References

[1] *Worlds Before Our Own*, Brad Steiger (W. H. Allen, 1980).

[2] ibid.

[3] ibid.

[4] ibid.

[5] ibid.

[6] *The Hot-blooded Dinosaurs*, Adrian J. Desmond (Futura, 1977).

[7] *Mysteries of Time & Space*, Brad Steiger (Prentice Hall, 1974).

[8] *There Are Giants in the Earth*, Michael Grumley (Sidgwick & Jackson, 1975).

[9] ibid.

[10] ibid.

[11] 'A Funny Thing Happened (on the way to extinction)', C. A. O'Conner, *The UFO Debate*, Vol. 2, No. 6, Dec. 1991.

[12] *In Search of Ancient Mysteries*, A. & S. Lansburg (Corgi, 1974).

[13] ibid.

[14] *Secrets of the Lost Races*, René Noorbergen (Bobbs-Merrill, 1977)

[15] ibid.

[16] *Our Ancestors Came From Outer Space*, Maurice Chatelain (Dell, 1979).

[17] *Chariots of the Gods?*, Erich von Daniken (Souvenir Press, 1969).

[18] Noorbergen, op. cit.

[19] *Gods & Spacemen in the Ancient East*, W. Raymond Drake (Sphere, 1973).

[20] Steiger (1974), op. cit.

[21] Noorbergen, op. cit.

[22] ibid.

[23] ibid.

[24] ibid.

[25] *Understanding Mu*, Hans Stefan Santesson (Paperback Library, 1970).

[26] Steiger (1974), op. cit.

[27] ibid.

[28] *Timeless Earth*, Peter Kolosimo (Sphere, 1974).

CHAPTER 4
Moonshines

O F ALL the generations of humankind that I might have lived in, I count myself lucky to be part of the one that was to see the science fiction of its youth turned into reality before it reached middle age – a time when humankind went from being a purely planetary phenomenon to achieving the potential for inhabiting the Universe at large. In the decades in the middle of this century, science fact caught up with science fiction and, courtesy of the television in nearly every living-room, everybody went to the Moon.

The Moon has always exercised a strong fascination for humankind. In fact, 'For most, if not all, of the human experience, the moon has been regarded as a mysterious and powerful entity. It has been worshipped and feared and consulted.'[1] So strong is its actual influence that many natural cycles owe their periodicity to its phases and orbital influence. The face of the man in the Moon is a familiar illustration in childhood fairy-tales, and we soon learned of its romantic connotations as we sailed the stormy seas of puberty. It had a special place in humankind's dreams of space conquest. Jules Verne, H.G. Wells and a host of movies in the same vein as *Destination Moon* testify to this. Then, one day in July 1969, all the science fiction became science fact and humankind made the 'one giant leap' to the Moon. By the time American astronauts were turning the lunar surface into the first interplanetary junkyard, public expectations of the seemingly unstoppable arrival of the 'space age' were running high. Surely now, we thought – or hoped – the many questions that had waited aeons would at last be answered. But then came the anti-climax, because any answers were drowned in the torrent of new questions that the Moon missions generated, and their almost inexplicable cancellation before they had fully run their course. What did the Americans meet up there that persuaded them to relinquish the prize that had been coveted by humankind for generations, and for which they and their Russian rivals had worked so hard for to reach first?

On the face of it, the Moon should have held few surprises for those intrepid astronauts who stepped on its surface. After all, according to science it was airless and uninhabited. Why then, from the outset, were there hints of an anomalous presence there? Even before the first landing in 1969, while Apollo 8 was on its first Moon orbit, its crew reported sighting a 'disc shaped object'.[2] At the same time, the crew found their spaceship inexplicably pitching and yawing, while the cabin temperature climbed alarmingly and they were subjected to a blinding light: 'Moreover, from time to time through these weird experiences they heard strange radio noises which they described alternately as "intolerable high frequency noises" and "weird garble".'[3] These alleged events inspired Otto Binder, a respected science writer with NASA, to speculate that UFOs had tried to prevent Apollo 8 from orbiting the Moon. In which case, that particular ploy can be said to have failed. In the end, however, something on the Moon did send the American space programme scuttling for cover. Could it have been aliens, or something even more startling?

In considering the possibilities for an inhabited Moon, we have three obvious choices. An indigenous population composed of born and bred Selenites? An extraterrestrial task force using the Moon as a forward base for observing/invading Earth? A population composed of the descendants of those who were trapped up there when the 'sudden' Cretaceous cataclysm made impossible their return to Earth? The first option can be dispensed with on the grounds that native selenites are fine in Wellsian fiction, but present too many practical problems for them to have lived unobserved on the Moon for as long as humankind has had it under scrutiny. The second option, while quite attractive at first glance, has to be rejected because LTP (lunar transient phenomena) have been reported by competent observers for over 500 years, and in all that time there has been no observable strategic build-up. In any case, the logistics of any such operation preclude its possibility almost from the outset. These eminently rational reasons should have meant that the

Moon was uninhabited until the *Eagle* landed; but there is still a legacy of ongoing evidence that annoyingly argues for some kind of life there prior to the American astronauts' arrival. This is strongly circumstantial evidence that should be taken seriously, because 'nearly all of the early observers are known to have been scientists of integrity'.[4] And that leaves only option three to account for any alien (non-human, but not necessarily extra-terrestrial) presence on the Moon.

If, as has been speculated in the previous chapters, the dinosaur species did produce an intelligent race, like Dr Dale A. Russell's, which had achieved an interplanetary capability, what would have happened to them when the great extinction occurred at the end of the Cretaceous period? Would they, caught by surprise, have gone the way of all flesh? Or, being intelligent, would they have foreseen what would happen and made contingency plans? The probability is that the cataclysm (especially a nuclear war) started so unexpectedly that only those in privileged positions would have had any chance of survival, some, perhaps, in purpose-built bunkers, and others at instal-lations at the Poles; some in bases on the Moon, and others, perhaps, on missions in deep space. There might have been some on Mars who, before they died for lack of supplies, left a recognizable message for any subsequent 'search and rescue' mission. In view of the sheer scale of the cataclysm that cut them off from Earth, it is probable that no rescuers ever came, but intriguingly, 'In July of 1976 one of NASA's Viking Orbiters acquired an image of what appeared to be a humanoid face staring straight out into space from the surface of Mars.'[5] It is all speculation, of course, but without knowing the precise details of the Earth-shaking events that closed the Cretaceous period, that's all there is. Science speculates all the time on the basis of even less convincing circumstantial evidence and nobody objects, so let us continue and see if anything can be deduced from our speculations to clarify more immediate mysteries.

LTP have been reported sporadically over the centuries by astronomers of the stature of Sir John Herschel, Rev. Nevil Maskelyne (the Astronomer Royal) and other equally acceptable astronomical observers, but particularly in the late 1800s. It seems almost as if a static indigenous population had suddenly been augmented and re-energized, and a new sense of urgency had thereby been injected into efforts to contact colleagues on Earth. The burst of LTP began in 1869, and it is still unexplained some 22 years after the last Moon landing by Apollo 17. Before it ceased in 1870, over 2,000 observations of anomalous light effects on the Moon had been observed and logged by observatories around the world. Night after night, with a persistence that intrigued the observers, these mystery lights 'appeared singly, in circular groups, triangular and straight formations; *moving* and *varying* in intensity as if they were under intelligent control'.[6] So strong was this impression that attempts were undertaken to decipher a message from what appeared to be coded configurations. It was hoped that the lights might represent extraterrestrial efforts at cosmic communication; a hope that was reinforced by the fact that the lights did not just appear randomly on the Moon's surface, but they were concentrated in the vicinity of the Mare Crisium. Regrettably, contact was not established, and the lights 'went out' as suddenly and mysteriously as they had been 'switched on'. Such is the inbred anthropocentricism of the human race, especially in those days, that it never occurred to anyone to ask if the 'messages' might have been directed at a life form other than the human race – intelligent dinosaur survivors, for instance. The light effects could have ceased because the desired contact had been made. Strange lunar lights were observed again in 1877. The new outbreak began in February and, although as intriguing as those of 1869, the lights were not as numerous or as geometric. Professor H. Harrison reported in June 1877 that he had seen a light on the Moon which 'looked very much like the reflection from a moving mirror'.[7] However, it was not inferred that it was an attempt at communication by an alien life form on the Moon. Even so, private suspicions, perhaps even apprehensions, that the Moon was not quite as 'dead' as it ought to have been grew as the world moved into the twentieth century. From 1927 to 1934, even on the primitive equipment in use at that time, radio signals were received from the Moon. Then in 1935, 'Two scientists named Van der Pol and Stormer detected radio signals on or around the Moon.'[8] It might be seen as somewhat synchronous that these were the same two scientists who were to draw attention later to the anomalous nature of the so-called 'auroral display' of 25 January 1938 – an event which also has a probable UFO conection. So as the twentieth century advanced and radio-receiving equipment improved, 'signals' continued to be received from the Moon. In 1956 the University of Ohio, in common with other organizations around the world, reported receiving 'code like radio chatter from the Moon'.[9] An even more evidential event occurred in October 1958, when:

> American, Soviet and British Astronomers detected something speeding toward the Moon at better than 25,000 miles per hour. They not only saw the strange object; they heard it emitting radio signals that no one could interpret![10]

Thus, by the time UFOs had made their ineradicable impression on the public consciousness, the general ufological concensus regarding the importance of LTP was encapsulated by Donald Keyhoe when he wrote, 'All the evidence suggested not only the existence of a moon base, but that operations by an intelligent race have already begun.'[11] He, of course, was writing in an 'ET is upon us' context. However, his conclusion about operations by an intelligent race is even more interesting when looked at alongside evidence of the survival of the race of intelligent dinosaurs.

Throughout the 1950s LTP diversified into other, and even more evidential, forms. For instance, during the night of 23 July 1953, the then science editor of the *Herald Tribune*, J.J. O'Neil, saw on the Moon something resembling a huge 'bridge', spanning 12 miles (19 km), in the Mare Crisium, in the same area as the 'light show' of 1869. When he reported his sighting, he was immediately set upon by professional astronomers, who discounted his observation on the grounds that, having looked at this area many times themselves, they had never seen anything like the construction described by him. Fortunately for O'Neil, his debunkers were discomfited when no lesser a figure than the British astronomer H.P. Wilkins (then considered to be the premier lunar authority) confirmed the existence of the bridge in the Mare Crisium, calling it 'one of the most amazing, mysterious and artificial looking features on the Moon'.[12] Once the existence of this 'artificial looking' anomaly was attested to in this way, other astronomers, including Patrick Moore, joined in the chorus of confirmation. Even its apparent artificiality was never seriously called into question. In a radio interview, H.P. Wilkins responded to a question about the 'bridge' by stating, 'It looks artificial.'[13]

When challenged to define what he meant by 'artificial', he went on to say, 'Well, it looks almost like an engineering job.'[14] You can't say fairer than that, even though it leaves begging the question of who built it? Neil Armstrong's 'one small step' was still well in the future, so the opportunity to find an answer had to wait. In the event, throughout all the Moon landings, the question was never apparently addressed. Had it been forgotten? There is evidence to suggest otherwise.

There might be those who still think that had there been anything untoward on the Moon, the human race would have heard about it through the seemingly 'live' transmissions from the Apollo spacecraft from the Moon's surface, which continued after landings. In actual fact, Mission Control had a built-in ten second delay in transmission which enabled it to censor any incoming material. Also, when astronaut transmissions were broadcast, it was possible to suspect that a code, to which the general public was not privy, was in use between the astronauts and Mission Control. According to an article in *Saga* magazine, the use of a code was practically admitted by Dr Farouk El Baz, a NASA scientist, when he was asked to clarify a point raised by a nonsensical reference to 'Barbara' during a conversation between astronaut Young on the Moon and Mission Control on Earth:

> *Saga*: What do you suppose Young meant when he said they came upon 'Barbara'?
> *El Baz*: I can't really say. Code, perhaps . . ..
> *Saga*: But Barbara is an odd name for something on the Moon, isn't it?
> *El Baz*: Yes, an enigma. As I suggested, perhaps a code, but I don't really know.[15]

Yet even with such surreptitious censorship procedures in place, enough information eventually surfaced to put beyond reasonable doubt the probability that *every* Apollo mission encountered UFOs while in transit and on the Moon. But what of that bridge? Apparently, orbital photographs of the Mare Crisium taken from Apollo 16 in April 1972 showed 'several "bridges"'.[16] So it might seem that some questions have been answered in the affirmative, and the only mystery remaining is why this discovery has not been noised in the media. As Dr Farouk El Baz has admitted: 'Not every discovery has been announced.'[17] Why not? Could it have been because the 'bridges' and other unadmitted lunar 'constructions' were so obviously 'cyclopean', after the fashion of Tiuhanaco and Baalbek, that they confirmed what had been suspected since 1947: that there is another life form, superior to humankind, native to planet Earth, entrenched upon the Moon?

Looking back, it now seems unsurprising that the Moon landings only compounded the existing mystery. Even the overt reasons given for initiating the space programme might have been untrue, and the American Establishment 'did not spend billions to reach something merely it is "there"'.[18] Clearly, there was a hidden agenda from the outset. The ten-second delay and the exisence of a clandestine code proclaims this with certainty. Both these facilities were probably in place during the Gemini missions, so they clearly indicate an unacceptable degree of premeditation on the part of NASA. Why incorporate such censorship into Moon mission communications and then give the public the erroneous impression of uncensored spontaneity? What gave NASA the idea that such facilities might be needed? What did they *plan* to keep from the public?

Inexorably, the above questions bring us back to the ufological accusation of an 'Establishment cover-up' in relation to anything to do with UFOs. That there was something kept from the public during the Apollo missions is easily demonstrated by the unequivocal assertions made by Maurice Chatelain, an ex-NASA scientist:

> It seems that all Apollo and Gemini flights were followed, both at a distance but also sometimes quite closely, by space vehicles of extra-terrestrial origin – flying saucers, or UFOs (Unidentified Flying Objects), if you want to call them by that name. Every time it occurred, the astronauts informed Mission Control, who then ordered absolute silence.[19]

Equally another former NASA scientist, Dr F. Bell, claimed to have seen photographs of UFOs taken by astronauts. He said, 'The astronauts have kept silent about their UFO encounters because they are trained to believe it is a matter of national security.'[20] What is a 'matter of national security'? The existence of extraterrestrials? Probably not, because the human race can accept the existence of 'space aliens' since they are a theme in our literary culture. But are we as prepared for a confrontation with those who 'bred' us? And who could – if called upon to do so – demonstrate how they bred a multi-purpose bio-robot that could be cheaply and quickly produced by unskilled labour – especially by unskilled labour. All they have to do now is remove the genetic glitch that predisposed their otherwise excellent bio-servo mechanism to ego malfunction (i.e., disobedience, rebellion). Such a failing was the real 'original sin', not sex, because it is obvious that we were bred to reproduce in order to mass produce replacements for those who succumbed to that original expression of the concept of 'planned obsolescence' (i.e., death). Now, *that* would really be a 'saucer secret' worth the keeping.

The Apollo Moon missions were stopped quite suddenly after Apollo 17. Despite the technology to do so, they have not been resumed. The enforced cessation of manned Moonshoots was quite unexpected, and, 'Many serious scientists were disappointed at the discontinuation of the Apollo program which ended abruptly with the Apollo 17 flight.'[21] The cessation seemed highly strange if you remember the ballyhoo that preceded, then accompanied, America's successful attempts to put a man on the Moon. It was implied at the time of cancellation that lack of finance was the problem. Yet, stopping the programme at Apollo 17 wasted more money than if the programme had continued as envisaged. The whole series of Moon landings individually, and collectively, had seemed an incredible success. Nevertheless, they ended anticlimactically, and they were rarely mentioned again in the media. Were they the failure that the general public was now encouraged to feel they were, or could they have been too successful in that 'we found too much up there. That is the reason we stopped so abruptly.'[22] As might be expected, the sudden cancellation of the Apollo programme provoked much ufological speculation about alien task forces. These were given added impetus by the startling statements from ex-NASA scientists who more or less said aliens *were* on the Moon – just what the UFO buffs wanted to hear. But just consider this. If, as is always ufologically implied, governments really want to suppress information about UFOs being extraterrestrial vehicles, it is highly unlikely that scientists whose jobs depended on government grants would risk making statements that could be taken as admissions that the ET hypothesizers were correct. After all, as government employees, particularly during their tenure at

NASA, they must have had to get security clearance. To gain this, they must have signed the relevant secrecy acts, ensuring that the Establishment had ample means to silence them if necessary. In this context, it can only be seen as synchronously sinister that the first proponent of the 'invading aliens' thesis was himself another 'retired' Establishment type, Major Donald E. Keyhoe. When looked at carefully, it can be seen that he single-handedly introduced and proselytized the ET Hypothesis, thus initiating the highly entertaining confrontation that has probably kept generations of ufologists chasing chimeras while the real 'UFO secret' remained inviolate.

There is little doubt that the entire American space program was, at bottom, a military enterprise and not a civilian one as the public was led to believe: 'It seems that most of the public was never aware that Secretary of Defense Forrestal announced the U.S. satellite program in 1948.'[23] The probability is that the race for the Moon was the culmination of a military strategy hastily initiated in 1947 for reasons that will be made clear in a later chapter. However, for the moment, it is sufficient to indicate that not only were the American astronauts looking for something on the Moon, they knew precisely what it was. Hence the use of specific 'identification codes' in ground control/astronaut conversations. For instance, during the final Apollo 17 flight, when the command module pilot in orbit round the Moon reported a 'flashing light' in Crater Orientale:

> Whether or not it is true that Houston took it calmly, they did seem to insist on switching to some pre-arranged code: KILO KILO. They then continued to use these various possible code words from then on: BRAVO, BRAVO, SELECT OMNI.[24]

However, the high visibility of this anomaly indicates that whatever is on the Moon did not give a damn if it was seen by the astronauts. Understand this in the context of unconcern at our being watched by animals and you might get an inkling of why governments have gone to extreme lengths to keep what they know secret. Even so, there is an apocryphal story regarding the first Moon landing. It is clearly in the area of cosmic conjecture, because it is unauthenticated by NASA – not surprisingly. According to Otto Binder, people could bypass NASA's broadcast delay and pick up startling exchange between Aldrin and

Armstrong and Mission Control at Houston. These would have been edited out of any rebroadcast to the media. There are several versions extant, the fullest, and perhaps the most questionable, version appeared in *The National Bulletin*, a weekly newspaper widely circulated in Canada and the USA.[25] However, according to Binder the officially denied exchange started when Aldrin and Armstrong were moonwalking some distance from the LEM. Apparently, Armstrong said:

> What was it, what the Hell was it? That's all I want to know . . ..
>
> There followed further snatches of gasping interchanges between the two Astronauts with Mission Control also chiming in frantically.
>
> *Mission Control*: What's there? . . . malfunction [garble] . . . Mission Control calling Apollo eleven . . ..
>
> *Apollo 11*: These babies were huge, sir . . . Enormous . . . Oh God, you wouldn't believe it! [What could Apollo 11 be referring to?] I'm telling you there are other spacecraft out there . . . lined up on the far side of the crater edge . . . they're on the Moon watching us . . .[26]

If this exchange is spurious, why would Binder risk his reputation by referring to it? If true, even if only in essence, would it explain why Armstrong is allegedly living as a recluse some 25 years after the Moon landing during which he possibly had this experience? It is of some interest that whatever was 'watching' was referred to familiarly as 'they', and not 'space aliens' or any other designation that would indicate the unexpected presence of non-terrain life forms. This, in turn, might indicate that the Apollo 11 astronauts had stumbled upon something that was at least half expected and known to be from planet Earth, but which still managed to surprise them by its presence on the Moon. However, from the consuming disinterest in the Moon since the end of the Apollo programme, one would be hard pressed to understand the original excitement and anticipation generated by it. Most people now seem to think that it was a waste of time and effort. The public are not openly encouraged to understand that more questions than answers were generated by the Moon landings and that, according to Patrick Moore in *Omni* magazine, 'In our present phase of post-Apollo enlightenment, it would be wrong to suggest that all the mysteries of the Moon have been solved.'[27]

Were *any* mysteries solved? Reading the latest astronomical literature on the subject, one would be tempted to think not. Certainly, the mystery of LTP remains, even though the Apollo mission had ample opportunity to investigate it. Or, could it be that the mystery has been solved and that those who know are now faced with the problems of how to break the bad news to humanity? Why do I think it is bad news? Well, if it were good news every politician on Earth would now be claiming credit for it, and in this context I find Establishment silence deafening. Logically, it can be deduced that something caused all those LTP, which are still going on. Since the LTP were visible from Earth, they should have been obvious to astronauts on the lunar surface and their companion in the orbiting command module. Certainly, all the Apollo missions reported seeing LTP. Apollo 11 heard unexplained radio transmissions; Apollo 12 was hit by a 'bolt of lightning' during take off, even though the weather people reported that the nearest lightning was miles away. Then after a UFO-haunted trip to the Moon it was met by the now almost obligatory anomalous radio transmissions. And so it went on all through the Apollo programme, with the pilot in the command module of Apollo 16 seeing a 'flash' on the side of Descartes. Then came Apollo 17, and

> When command module pilot Ronald Evans reported the object he saw with flashing lights on the eastern edge of Orientale Crater, Houston asked, observes *Saga* reporter Joseph Goodavage, 'You don't suppose it could be a Vostok?'[28]

More likely it was that London bus I have heard so much about, because, 'Who'd ever expect to find an obsolete Russian spaceship (one that wasn't supposed to be able to reach the Moon in the first place) sitting in a lunar crater flashing its lights?'[29] But be not deceived (as I think we were supposed to be) by the seemingly jocular reference to Vostok.

Something serious was being discussed, as indicated by the previous instructions that Ronald Evans should 'go to KILO'. His reply about the Mode going to HM; the recorder being off; his statement, 'there's BRAVO, BRAVO' and that Houston should select OMNI: why talk in such riddles if you have no intention to conceal? Is it possible that the real truth was indicated by the quotation that was chosen to preface the Apollo 17 Preliminary Science Report:

> There is nothing more difficult to take in hand, or perilous to conduct, or more uncertain in its success, than to take the lead in the introduction of a new order of things.[30]

Could this refer to the new world order we have all heard so much about of late? Perhaps not, because if the thesis of this book is correct, then what was found on the Moon could indicate the probable return of a very old world order – prehistoric probably.

References

[1] *The Lunar Effect*, Arnold L. Lieber M. D., produced by Jerome Agel (Corgi, 1979).

[2] *Our Mysterious Spaceship Moon*, Don Wilson (Sphere, 1976).

[3] ibid.

[4] ibid.

[5] *The Martian Enigmas*, Mark J. Carlotto (North Atlantic Books, 1991).

[6] Wilson, op. cit.

[7] 'Alien Saucers on the Moon', Philip Asher, *UFO Debate*, No. 1.

[8] Wilson, op. cit.

[9] ibid.

[10] ibid.

[11] *Flying Saucer Conspiracy*, Donald Keyhoe (Holt, 1955).

[12] *Our Moon*, H. P. Wilkins (Frederick Muller, 1954).

[13] *Secrets of Our Spaceship Moon*, Don Wilson (Sphere, 1980).

[14] ibid.

[15] Wilson, op. cit.

[16] *Someone Else is on Our Moon*, George H. Leonard (Sphere, 1978).

[17] Wilson (1976), op. cit.

[18] Leonard, op. cit.

[19] *Our Ancestors Came From Outer Space*, Maurice Chatelain (Pan, 1980)

[20] Asher, op. cit.

[21] *We Discovered Alien Bases on the Moon*, Fred Steckling (GAF International, 1981).

[22] ibid.

[23] *Moongate: Suppressed Findings of the U.S. Space Program*, William L. Brian II (Future Science Research Publishing, 1982).

[24] Wilson (1976), op. cit.
[25] *Fate* (Athol Publications, March 1971).
[26] Wilson (1976), op. cit.
[27] Steckling, op. cit.
[28] Wilson (1976), op. cit.
[29] ibid.
[30] Leonard, op. cit.

CHAPTER 5
Byrd of Ill Omen?

FROM almost the very beginning of the 'UFO Age', in 1947, there have been two claims made by UFO buffs that make not the slightest sense in the context of extraterrestrial interference on Earth. Interestingly, though, the same claims would be unremarkable – almost expected, indeed – in context of the possible survival of an intelligent dinosaur race. The two claims, which are now part of the ufological orthodoxy that supports the logically insupportable ET Hypothesis, are that UFOs (meaning spaceships) were attracted to this planet by the detonation of the atom bomb in 1945, and – based on the content of alleged abductee/contactee adventures – that ETs came to warn us of the perils of plutonium, and because they feared that our dalliance with doomsday weaponry might 'upset the balance of the Universe'. Contacteeism was the original setting for these ideas, incorporating as it did the notion of 'spacebrothers', who, synchronistically, seemed similar in almost all respects to the 'hidden Chiefs' of Blavatskian theosophy, the 'guides' of spiritualism and the 'Angels/Demons' of classic Judeo-Christianity. The whole of the contactee 'spacebrothers will save us' scenario, from Adamski's Venusians onward, could have been dismissed as being the activities of those who preyed for profit, after the fashion of the bogus 'psychics' and 'mediums' of earlier generations, upon the nuclear fears of the cosmologically gullible. However, similar themes eventually emanated from the more seemingly 'scientific' abductee adventures. The inbuilt attractiveness of these science-fantasy scenarios is due in large part to the usual human egomania – individual and racial – and in part to the unwarranted ufological acceptance of the occult assumption that the human race will somehow be 'evolved' into some kind of ill-defined superbeing by contact with 'Cosmic Masters'. Just watch one of David Attenborough's excellent wildlife TV documentaries to understand why such anthropocentic ideas are unlikely to reflect reality. If UFOs exist – and they do – then whatever drives around in them will be pursuing its own purposes – not ours. So if UFO occupants express concern over our mismanagement of the Earth's ecosystem, then you can be sure it is because their own well being is intimately concerned; logically, that can only stem from them being as dependent on Earth for their continued existence as we are.

To argue convincingly that a race of intelligent dinosaurs survived to modern times, you must show that there is a case for the ongoing existence of an anomalous presence on planet Earth throughout the millennia that followed the Cretaceous catastrophe. You also have to indicate where the possible saurian survivalists could have remained hidden while recovering from the disaster that robbed their race of its pre-eminent place in the Earth's ecosystem. To find evidence of this anomalous 'non-human' presence on the Earth, all one needs to do is read the Bible and other sacred scripts. There is enough circumstantial material in the Old Testament alone to put beyond reasonable doubt the probability of a non-human, but not necessarily extraterrestrial, interference in our affairs on this planet. There is, of course, more secular evidence, some of it in the form of cave paintings, like the ones found in France, which depict UFO-type shapes. In one notable instance, discussed by Aimé Michel in an article in *Flying Saucer Review*, the palaeolithic painting 'depicts human beings chasing an alien being. The being is dark, has pointed features and slant eyes'.[1] That this strange 'alien being' should resemble the 'intelligent dinosaur' modelled by Dr Dale Russell must be more than merely synchronistic. However, you are entitled to ask: If such a dinosaur did survive, where did it keep itself hidden? Forgetting for the moment the easy options of bases on the Moon and Mars, and the crews of spaceships caught in interstellar space when the Cretaceous cataclysm occurred, we must look for a way that a remnant of such a race could have survived on Earth itself. In this context it can only be seen as significant that 'from all over the world there have come reports of underground caverns, tunnel systems, or even underground cities'.[2] These are just the kind of thing we have constructed to protect our élite from the nuclear consequences of their global politicking. So if such aides to survival can occur to us, why not to others? In fact, the atomic element aside, 'A supertechnological civilization could have built systems of tunnels for trading purposes and so on.'[3] In view of this, is it not significant that since time immemorial there has existed a reasonably coherent body of myths concerning a 'hidden kingdom', named variously as Agharti, Schamballah or Belovodye? Although, for the most part, these myths are unspecific about its location, all of them seems to agree that it is underground and that one day its inhabitants will resurface at the dawn of a 'new world order'?

Accepting for the sake of argument that 'where there's Foo there's fire', it can then be asked why did the possibility that the Earth might be hollow and contain lands inhabited by races unsuspected by surface humankind only really catch the public imagination with the publication of 'I Remember Lemuria' by Richard S. Shaver? It appeared in the March 1945 edition of the pulp science-fiction magazine *Amazing Stories*, which was edited at that time by Ray Palmer, who was later to specialize in ufology and kindred subjects. On the face of it, Shaver's story was typical of the pulp offerings of the day in which it was published. It deviated only in the device of bringing its BEMs (bug-eyed monsters) from inside the Earth rather than from outer space. Yet, it was this unremarkable literary device that eventually led to the events that caused what *Life* magazine described as 'the most celebrated mystery to rock the science fiction world'. The issue containing the Shaver story had hardly hit the news-stands before letters began arriving on the editor's desk from people claiming to have had experiences which proved that Shaver's subterranean villains were fact and not fiction. The affair reached such proportions that it cost Palmer his job, and resulted in the *Life* article quoted earlier appearing in May 1951. It is perhaps a tribute to the power of the human imagination that when the article was published, 'The reader response was overwhelming and the feature created more interest than any other articles *Life* had published up to that time.'[4] With hindsight, it is possible to argue that Shaver's story touched a previously unsuspected raw nerve in the human psyche, that darkened chamber of the mind wherein lurk all our archetypal cultural bogeymen. If that is not the case, then the story did possess an unexpected element of truth. The public reaction is therefore based on the probability that 'some long forgotten memory of the inner Earth still persists in the subconscious minds of people today'.[5] Whatever the truth of the matter, the 'Shaver mystery' only achieved occult immortality when it was subsequently realized by UFO researchers that certain of the vehicles used by Shaver's beings uncannily resembled the descriptions of flying saucers given to them. In fact, the Shaver mystery 'contained, in embryo, all the elements of today's Ufology, including the alleged hardware and the tendency to abduction for sexual purposes'.[6] Such a strange correlation can only mean one of two things: either the UFO phenomenon and the Shaver Mystery are both based on human delusions; or both are real and represent humankind's view of something which strongly argues for there being an unsuspected enemy somewhere on, or even inside, the planet.

Strange to tell, 'I Remember Lemuria' was not the first time that fiction about a race that lived inside the Earth was apparently taken for fact. There is evidence to indicate that the novel *The Coming Race* by George Bulwer Lytton was apparently the explanation for some otherwise inexplicable actions on the part of Hitler's Reich. No doubt, the attraction for the Nazis was the novel's emphasis on a 'superior' race of beings, and of the power wielded by them. Bulwer Lytton called it 'Vril' and credited it with the kind of clout that individuals capable of creating Nazism found irresistibly attractive, so much so that 'Hitler and his henchmen launched several unsuccessful expeditions to the hollow earth.'[7] Mad though the idea might now appear, there is no doubt that the Reich was modelled on the utopianism (suitably Nazified) that permeated Bulwer Lytton's novel. This is the same kind of unworkable utopianism that now seems to be endemic in the Universe, if the statements of the 'aliens' to their contactee/abductees are to be believed. Despite what mainstream historians have made of the Nazi adventure, it would seem that the Nazis were pursuing a hidden occult agenda, as demonstrated by the fact that as Hitler's armies swept into Czechoslovakia in 1939 'a special group of S.S. men were ordered into the defeated country'.[8] This élite group was under the supervision of Himmler and its avowed purpose was to investigate the truth of the 'inner earth' legends they had collected from all over Europe, in particular from Czechoslovakia. That the operation was unsuccessful should surprise nobody, because the beliefs on which it was based apparently derived in large measure from a fictional account of a non-existent civilization. It would be comforting to think so, but there are hints that Himmler was perhaps unlucky in his search and that there possibly was something to be found after all. In an article called 'A Remarkable Underground Grotto', published in *National Speleological Society News* in 1965, Dr Antonin Horak describes a singularly synchronistic experience which befell him while he was a resistance fighter in, of all places, German-occupied Czechoslovakia. Apparently, Horak was fleeing with a wounded companion after an engagement with the enemy when a group of local peasants helped him to the safety of a cave. As they left, they warned him not to go deep into the cave because there were pockets of lethal gas. The cave was also 'haunted'. The speleologist in Dr Horak could not resist the temptation to explore. After crawling through various passageways, he found himself confronting a large, dark, silo-like cylinder. It seemed to be man made and about 80 ft (24 m) in diameter. Inside, Horak used his torch to see 'a spacious, curved, black shaft formed by cliff like walls'. Horak says his find reminded him of legends relating to lost civilizations with magic technologies. Could it be that he had inadvertently stumbled upon the very thing Himmler so unsuccessfully searched for . . . an entrance to the 'hidden kingdom'? If so, then he wasn't the only one: Alec Maclellan, while holidaying in the Yorkshire Dales, apparently came across a similar entrance. Initially thinking he was only exploring one of the many caves that abound in the area, he was very soon disabused of that notion when he became aware of a 'pulsating' green light in the tunnel ahead of him. This was eventually accompanied by a 'humming' sound which gave Maclellan the distinct impression that 'something' was coming towards him. Eventually, the growing intensity of the strange green light and the humming – which had become a 'rumble' that vibrated through the tunnel floor – forced him to flee. Of his untoward experience, Maclellan had this to say:

> The eerie green light was unlike any I had ever seen before, and the rumbling sound had almost seemed as if it came from some huge piece of machinery. Could the one have been an underground light and the other some strange subterranean means of transport?[10]

And what if it were exactly as Maclellan speculated? The inescapable corollary must be that strange though any subterranean means of transport might seem to us, it must fulfil the purpose of any transport: to convey persons and goods from one place to another. In which case, we must ask: who or what was Maclellan's underground transport taking where? The 'hidden kingdom'? Surely not, because twentieth-century science has now explored everything and left no room for products of pre-scientific mythologies? Or has it?

When it comes to the composition of the interior of the Earth, science seems somewhat unsure. For long enough it was taught that the core of our planet was molten, and much 'incontrovertible' evidence was offered in scientific support of this contention. Lately, though, current scientific thinking contends that the Earth's core is solid, and once again 'impeccable' scientific evidence is produced in support of this hypothesis. Perhaps, in view of science's ability to 'prove' conclusively, in the space of one generation, two mutually exclusive conditions at Earth's core, we can forgive those who seek elsewhere for evidence to either support or demolish the truth of a secret underground civilization. So far, it is possible to accept the existence of a global network of tunnels similar to those found and explored by Soviet archaeologists which they believed:

> are part of a huge network stretching out towards Iran and perhaps linked with those discovered near the Amu Darya (in Turkmenistan on the Russo-Afghan border) or even the underground labyrinths of central and western China, Tibet and Mongolia.[11]

A tunnel network which could 'still afford refuge to the survivors of an immense cataclysm'.[12] Yet no matter how widespread these tunnel networks are demonstrated to be, they still are not sufficient to support a genuinely subterranean civilization similar to the fictional ones described by Bulwer Lytton and Shaver. Nonetheless, the old legends persist and they have been strengthened by the accruing evidence of a non-human presence on this planet as attested to by thousands of UFO witnesses. So is there something that conventional wisdom has missed? Or even deliberately ignored? Something which could fully explain the ongoing alien presence in more understandable terms than as an influx of aliens from seemingly every quarter of the known Universe?

At the turn of this century experiments were carried out by both the French and American Geodetic Survey Departments that produced results indicating that science was in serious error in respect of Copernican theory. All the experiments, originally initiated by France, were supposed to achieve was a more accurate determination of the actual size of the Earth. However, unable to believe their results, the French scientists requested their American counterparts to replicate the experiment to discover whether they had got it wrong. Unfortunately for all concerned, the Americans replicated the result. A pair of plumb bobs hung down mineshafts 4,270 ft (1,295 m) deep and 4,250 ft apart and connected by a transverse tunnel 4,250 ft long were 8¼ in (21 cm) further apart at the top than at the bottom. This divergence represented the exact divergence that would be necessary to complete a 360° circumference – a circle. It was bad enough to discover that Earth's centre of gravity was not where conventional science said it should have been, but that the circle indicated by the plumb lines 'would be the circumference of the *inside* of a sphere, and not the outside'.[13] Apparently this can only mean that either our present ideas about gravity are pure fantasy or that the earth is hollow – a speculation seemingly borne out by the photographs of the alleged North Polar opening taken by satellites ESSA–3 on 6 January 1967 and ESSA–7 on 23 November 1968.

Fortunately, there is more to go on in respect of the possibility of a hollow Earth than the allegedly suspect evidence of a couple of controversial satellite photographs. For instance, it has been known for some time that anomalies indicating the existence at the Poles of something more than a winter wasteland have been encountered by explorers: things like volcanic dust where there are no volcanoes; inexplicable warmth at latitudes where only sub-zero temperatures should exist; animal tracks in areas where there should be none apparently heading into areas even more inhospitable to life; and the fact that freshwater icebergs float south on the salty Arctic sea. Once you start looking, it is quite amazing how the mystery mounts until the only answer that will explain all the anomalies is that the Earth must be hollow. If this is so, why has it not been proved? The scientific literature of our day would seem to imply that planet Earth holds no such mystery, so what are we to believe? If it will help you to make up your mind, I am pleased to remind you that the scientific literature also does not admit to the existence of the UFOs. Do you suppose these two 'non-existent' mysteries could be interconnected in some way so that an admission of one is tantamount to the admission of the other . . . and more? I know that these days science has replaced religion as the arbiter of all things possible. In this context, you should bear in mind that religion resisted the incoming information that eventually rendered it useless as a yardstick for measuring reality. Perhaps the same is now about to happen to science. At one time dogmatic scientists scoffed at the 'non-scientific peasants' who said stones fell from the sky. Now scientists are falling over themselves to view a mountain chain descending on Jupiter, while at the same time they seek other stones in the sky that just might do the same to the Earth one day. Do not be convinced by science telling you that flying saucers do not exist and that even if they did, they could not come from inside the Earth. Perhaps, like the cardinals of Christianity, in defending their dogmas scientists are only trying to preserve their power base which, even as they speak, they feel crumbling beneath their feet. Anyway, who said the hollowness of the Earth has not been discovered? It has . . . a Dicky Byrd told me so.

Rear-Admiral Richard E. Byrd was a noted pioneer aviator. More importantly, in the context of our argument for a 'hidden kingdom' home for surviving intelligent dinosaur species which is also the base of the majority of UFOs, he was also a man obsessed by Polar exploration:

> The Encyclopedia Britannica states that on 9 May, 1926 Byrd and his co-pilot, Floyd Bennett, flew over the North Pole. Then on 29 November, 1929, with three companions he flew over the South Pole. In 1947 he made a second flight over the South Pole. finally, on 8 January, 1956, he flew over the South Pole for the third time.[14]

It must be remembered that these Polar overflights were an integral part of extensive expeditions which he led in those areas. Furthermore, the foregoing is only the 'official' version of his Polar activities. In the occult apocrypha he is credited with far more than just 'flying over' the North and South Poles. In many ways, the Polar discoveries credited to the Byrd expeditions in popular occult folklore provide not just a connection with the 'hidden kingdom' of global folklore, but an explanation of the mystery of UFOs. The synchronicities which surround the Byrd expeditions are singular in both number and content and probably clearly indicate why the Shaver stories – if indeed they were stories and not fact done up as fiction – shook the collective cultural psyche to its roots.

Looking at the 'official version', it is difficult to understand Byrd's obsession with Polar exploration. But if we accept the occult accusation that Byrd discovered that the Earth was hollow, then it becomes that much easier to understand why, just before his death in 1957, he referred to the object of his many expeditions as 'that enchanted continent in the sky, land of everlasting mystery'.[15] As might be expected, much has been read into those words. Predictably, there are some who insist they only make sense if taken in the context of Byrd, havin penetrated the Polar opening, seeing the inner Earth seemingly hanging above him in the sky. If these were the only inexplicable words uttered by Byrd in reference to his Polar explorations, they could be put down to poetic licence engendered by the onset of old age. However, they are not so easily dismissed, because they form part of a coherent body of remarks by Admiral Byrd that serve to strengthen the contention that his Polar explorations discovered more than has been admitted officially. In fact, here we find the real beginnings of the cover-up conspiracy so beloved of UFO buffs.

Astonishingly, Admiral Byrd's incredible Polar discoveries were apparently forgotten almost as soon as he had made them. It wasn't until the publication in 1959 of *Worlds Beyond the Pole* by Amadeo Giannini that any real attempt was made to bring them to the public's attention. Even then, as with the mystery to which Byrd's discoveries would become inextricably linked, there seems to have been persistent attempts by agencies unknown to suppress the book. Even as it was published, 'Giannini's book, for some strange reason, was not advertised by the publisher and remained unknown.'[16] In December 1959 the edition of the magazine *Flying Saucers* which carried information about Giannini's revelations 'disappeared':

As a result, 5000 subscribers did not get the magazine. One distributor who received 750 copies to sell on his newsstand was reported missing, and the 750 magazines disappeared with him.[17]

When the magazine's publisher, Ray Palmer (Shaver's 'I Remember Lemuria') attempted to get the printer to do a re-run, it was discovered that the plates were so badly damaged that no reprinting could be attempted. so, if skullduggery was involved, what was it keeping secret? The only thing that connects the book and the magazine are the references to Admiral Byrd's Polar explorations which had apparently ended in 1956 with the expedition that Byrd had announced in November 1955 as 'the most important expedition in the history of the world'.[18] This, you must admit, is a bit over the top, considering the orthodox view of where he was going. But what if the orthodox view is wrong . . . and *knowingly* wrong? Such a scenario would adequately explain not only any hollow Earth cover-up, but the UFO cover-up. Look at it this way, if during his 1926 and 1929 expeditions Byrd saw enough to suspect there was something strange at the Poles, he certainly confirmed those suspicions during his repeat performances in 1947 and 1956. By the time 1959 rolled around, the ETH mythology had been generated about UFOs in order to distract amateur investigators from the truth. The last thing the Establishment wanted was Byrd's discoveries made public, because this would have alerted the more perspicacious among the UFO community to re-evaluate their material and discover how they had been deliberately duped from the outset.

Let there be no doubt that the Byrd Polar expeditions did discover something strange. Byrd is credited with making public statements about his explorations that are difficult to understand in any context other than the disconcerting discovery of an entrance to unexpected lands inside the Earth. For instance, in 1947, prior to the expedition in which he allegedly flew for seven hours over lands *beyond* the North Pole, he is quoted as saying, 'I'd like to see that land beyond the Pole. That area beyond the pole is the centre of the great unknown.'[19] And in 1956, after returning from 'the most important expedition in the history of the world', he apparently claimed, 'The present expedition has opened up a vast new land.'[20] This claim can only have been based on the information given in an earlier radio broadcast, subsequently confirmed by the Press, that:

> Members of the United States expedition accomplished a flight of 2700 miles from the base at McMurdo Sound, which is 400 miles west of the South Pole, and penetrated a land extent of 2300 miles beyond the Pole.[21]

This is a neat trick, considering that there is not supposed to be enough land extent at the Pole to accommodate a penetration of 2,300 miles (4,345 km). Apparently, Admiral Byrd's expeditions were dogged by disinformation from the word go. The official version, as recorded in the *Encyclopaedia Britannica*, admits to only one expedition to the North Pole in 1926, and one to the South Pole in 1929. However, there are reasons for believing that Admiral Byrd overflew *both* poles in each of those years, because many people claim to have seen a news reel, narrated by Byrd himself, 'which described both flights, and also showed newsreel photographs of the "land beyond the pole" (north) with its mountains, trees, river, and a large animal identified as a mammoth'.[22] Ray Palmer claimed to have seen this documentary. Since it has now 'disappeared', debunkers can insinuate it was 'false memory' (as they similarly insinuate UFOs are 'misperceptions') on the part of the general public. W.A. Harbinson, discussing the topic in a two-part article in issues 27 and 28 of the partwork *The Unexplained*, dutifully echoed the official line when he wrote, 'Intriguing though this "short" would have been, there is no record of it now in any archive.'[23] Then, on the basis of this statement – which really only says that no copies of the film presently exist, and from which it cannot logically be presumed that the film never existed – Harbinson goes on to ask the rhetorical questions 'A U.S. Government cover-up? Or did the film ever really exist in the first place?'[24] . . . evidently presuming that the answer to both questions must be no. Using only his own data, it is obvious that the answers could just as easily be yes. Unfortunately, Harbinson then goes on to undermine his own argument – if blanket denials delivered *ex cathedra* can be said to constitute an argument – by quoting Byrd's own words from the October 1947 issue of *National Geographic Magazine*. According to this, Byrd wrote in his diary while circling the Pole in 1947: 'On the other side of the pole we are looking into that vast unknown area we have struggled so hard to reach.' Could he, as the debunkers would have us believe, really have been referring to more barren miles of snow and ice which he had seen at least once before, in 1929? In the light of his other recorded statement prior to his embarking on the 1947 Polar expedition, that he would 'like to see that land beyond the pole', wasn't he more likely to be referring to something a darn sight more interesting? Fortunately for us there is more to go on than the 'false memories' of the American public. Lloyd K. Grenlie was the radio man on Byrd's 1926 and 1929 Polar expeditions. In later life he was Ray Palmer's near neighbour, so forget 'false memory'. Ray Palmer got it 'from the radioman who went with Byrd to that land beyond the pole and *saw* the things recorded on film, that this unknown, uncharted, and presently denied land exists'.[25] And with that you can give sceptics the Byrd!

References

[1] *The Dark Gods*, Roberts and Gilbertson (Rider/Hutchison, 1980).
[2] ibid.
[3] ibid.
[4] *Secret of the Ages*, Brinsley le Poer Trench (Panther, 1976).
[5] ibid.
[6] *UFOs – The Final Answer?*, ed. David Barclay and Therese Marie Barclay (Blandford, 1993).
[7] *This Hollow Earth*, Warren Smith (Sphere, 1977).
[8] ibid.
[9] ibid.
[10] *The Lost World of Agharti*, Alec Maclellan (Souvenir Press, 1982).
[11] *Timeless Earth*, Peter Kolosimo (Sphere, 1974).
[12] ibid.
[13] le Poer Trench, op. cit.
[14] ibid.
[15] 'Fire Down Below?', D. Barclay, *The Unknown*, Aug. 1985.
[16] *The Hollow Earth*, Dr R. Bernard (Carol Paperbacks, 1991).
[17] ibid.
[18] ibid.
[19] le Poer Trench, op. cit.
[20] Barclay (1985), op. cit.
[21] ibid.
[22] le Poer French, op. cit.
[23] 'The Solid Facts', W. A. Harbinson, *The Unexplained*, Vol. 3, No. 28 (Orbis, 1981).
[24] ibid.
[25] Smith, op. cit.

CHAPTER 6

1947 That Was the Year, That Was!

WITH hindsight, which is always 20/20, it can be seen that 1947 was the beginning of the end for the world as it had been up to that time. In 1947 everyone imagined that life was going to return to what it was before the war broke out. No one was aware that up above the Arctic Circle an event had transpired to put an end to the familiar world. It would lead eventually to the creation and maintenance of a monumental mythology to protect people from that dreadful knowledge.

Apparently, about February 1947 Rear-Admiral Richard E. Byrd led an expedition to the Arctic during which he flew 'beyond' the North Pole for 1,700 miles (2,736 km), into an unmapped Polar depression or the entrance to 'inner Earth'. This expedition is now officially denied and it is implied that there was a flight on 16 February over the South Pole. Even then, the debunkers are left with Byrd's remarks about wanting to see the 'land beyond the pole', and of there being a 'vast unknown area' on the other side of the Pole, to explain unconvincingly, or rather explain away, as 'descriptive phrases' referring to the Polar area he must have already overflown in 1926 and 1929. However, debunkers seldom – if ever – refer to the fact that Admiral Byrd's North Polar flight of 1947 was reported in New York newspapers as it was happening:

> These accounts described Byrd's 1700-mile flight of seven hours over *land and fresh water lakes BEYOND* the assumptive North Pole "end" of the Earth. And the dispatches were intensified until *a strict censorship was imposed from Washington*.[1]

The cover-up that would eventually include flying saucers had begun.

Having been in ufology since before it 'officially' began in 1947, I am often appalled by the unwarranted assumption by newcomers to the mystery that all the aerial anomalies reported in the early days have been adequately explained. The truth of the matter is that hardly any of the seminal saucer sightings have been satisfactorily solved. In fact, there is much in early saucery that makes little sense unless you assume that the parameters of a cover-up were in place as early as 1929 but they were only activated in 1945, in anticipation of Admiral Byrd's return to Polar exploration after World War 2. It is possible that, at first, the innocent were used without their knowledge in some kind of intelligence exercise to test the cultural waters in regard to beliefs in superior subterranean civilizations? The subject was reduced to ridicule and received its social stigma by virtue of the public response to the 'Shaver Mystery'. Could Richard S. Shaver have been an intelligence operative and Ray Palmer his dupe? At this remove in time, who can tell? But having pulled a stunt like that once on Palmer and succeeded, perhaps whoever it was felt that there was no harm in doing the same to saucers. It has become almost an article of ufological faith that the study got its start with the report submitted by Kenneth Arnold in June 1947. Unfortunately, Arnold's report, and his subsequent behaviour, give rise to suspicions that he might have been an Establishment *agent provocateur* whose mission was to reduce to ridicule the subject of anomalous aircraft. It is a matter of public record that Kenneth Arnold reported 'flying wing'-type aeroforms. There is a photograph, still extant, showing him holding a drawing of a 'crescent-shaped' object and pointing to it as being a representation of the ones he reported seeing over the Cascades. This makes one ask why he later allowed Ray Palmer to publish in the first edition of *Fate* magazine an article entitled 'I Did See the Flying Disks'. And when the first UFO books were published, 'The smallest of these was a 16 page booklet by Kenneth A. Arnold entitled "The Flying Saucer As I Saw It".'[2] There was also the book on which he collaborated with Palmer, *The Coming of the Saucers*, so you tell me what he was playing at. Can such contradictions be understood by assuming that he did not see anything over the Cascades, but that in submitting a bogus report and subsequently writing conflicting accounts, he was in fact fulfilling his Intelligence assignment of making the subject of anomalous aeroforms look ridiculous? That Kenneth Arnold did have a clandestine connection with military Intelligence is argued by the fact that when he requested their assistance during his investigation of the 'Maury Island Hoax' (a ufological incident that predated his own alleged sighting by three days), the response he got from them was immediate. Two officers and 32 armed Marines responded to a call for investigative assistance from an apparently civilian ufologist. If you can make any sense out of that scenario, other than accepting that Arnold was some kind of Intelligence operative – and possibly a senior one – I would be interested to hear how. If further evidence of Arnold's Establishment affinities is needed, it can be pointed out that during an interview after he had abandoned his alleged 'investigation' of the Maury Island sightings, he told a reporter for the *Evening Post* of Philadelphia, 'At my home I have been visited by unseen entities whom I believe to be pilots of these weird disks.'[3] Arnold's reference to invisible entities, poltergeist-like activities and his use of the word 'weird' seem to indicate that his probable intention on that occasion was to connect UFOs with weirdos – an accepted Establishment disinformation strategy.

By mid-1947 it must have seemed to whoever was perpetrating the cover-up that everything was well in hand, and that they were succeeding in investing the interconnected subjects of anomalous aeroforms and hollow Earth with the kind of social stigma that relegates subjects to the realms of kooks and crackpots, thus effectively draining the possibility of them receiving serious scientific study or of even being thought worthy of after-dinner conversations. Then came the incident that ineluctably indicated to the cover-up conspirators that something more than patronizing blanket denials and explanations implying 'misperception' based on 'wishful thinking' by the more cosmologically gullible element of the general public was going to be needed to disinform effectively serious interest in flying saucers. In early July 1947, a flying saucer apparently crashed, or was brought down, in New Mexico. Although originally known as the 'Roswell Incident', the flying saucer did not crash at Roswell, the real sequence of events was that:

At about ten minutes to ten on the evening of 2 July 1947, local hardware dealer Dan Wilmot and his wife were sitting on the front porch of their South Penn Street home in Roswell, New Mexico, enjoying a cool respite from what had been one of those hot New Mexico summer days. In Wilmot's words, 'All of a sudden a big glowing object zoomed out of the sky from the south-east. It was going north-west [towards Corona, New Mexico] at a high rate of speed.'[4]

Then, before the object reached Corona, it was hit by 'something'. In the literature this has been claimed to be a 'lightning bolt' because, as the object passed across the area, there was a bad thunderstorm. Considering the proximity of White Sands Proving Grounds and Trinity Site, and that the object's observed direction of flight would eventually have taken it over Los Alamos, it could just as easily have been some kind of anti-aircraft projectile. Whatever the cause the result was that:

A great quantity of wreckage was blown out over the ground, but the saucer itself, although stricken, managed to remain in the air for at least long enough to get over the mountains.[5]

At that point, the shattered saucer's flight path became altered so that it travelled at right angles to its direction over Roswell. This modified flight path took it over Socorro (sound familiar?) and even closer to White Sands, as it passed over the Magdalena/San Mateo Mountains before crashing on the plains of San Agustin. Despite excellent detective work, initially by William Moore and Charles Berlitz, and subsequently even more painstaking enquiries by Stanton T. Friedman and Don Berliner, the so-called Roswell Incident has managed to maintain its aura of mystery. Even to this day the Establishment is able to assert – as it does with Byrd's 1947 North Polar expedition – that the crash never happened. And if you believe that, then you probably also believe that flying saucers are spaceships.

Fortunately for the Establishment, the crash occurred in a relatively uninhabited area that helped the hurried damage-limitation exercise that followed. That the 'crash' had probably been monitored on radar is supported by the alacrity with which the 'army' arrived at the site seemingly quite prepared for what it found – that is, a crashed saucer with its, probably but not necessarily dead, crew members. That no 'retrieval team' seems to have been similarly aware of the debris near Corona until alerted by the report made by 'Mac' Brazel also speaks volumes. As speedy as the damage limitation exercise was, it was too late to stop the wreckage of the main craft being viewed by civilians. A group of rockhunters, followed shortly by a group of archaeological students and their professor, allegedly found the saucer and spoke to at least one still-living crew member before the army arrived. According to Friedman and Berliner in *Crash at Corona*, the civilian witnesses noticed something that sounds a lot like modern fibre optics, in that there appeared to be electric cable hanging out of the damaged portion of the saucer – a cable composed of clusters of thread-like material and 'there were several hundred strands per one of these clusters . . . They blew in the wind like a horse's tail, except there was lights all over the ends of them.'[6] The similarity to modern fibre optics is emphasized when the witness says, 'They looked like fire on the ends of these thread-like things that were waving in the breeze.'[7] Fibre optics in 1947? More significant for the thesis of this book, the witness – although describing a living 'alien' which he took to be from 'space' – does not say that the creature was wearing a spacesuit. Apparently it was breathing our atmosphere as to the manner born. The leader of the second group to arrive, Dr Buskirk, tried to speak to the 'alien' in a number of languages, but got no response. It is clear from the dialogue reported by Friedman and Berliner that, despite the obvious absence of spacesuits and the fact that the still-living 'alien' must have tolerated New Mexico air and temperatures overnight, those civilians who were at the site when the army arrived in force were full of 'space alien' ideas. Perhaps, thereby hangs a tale.

While struggling, and succeeding, to keep a lid on the fact of a saucer crash on the plains of San Agustin, it must have occurred to those involved to wonder what would have happened if the saucer had crashed in a more populous area, like nearby Albuquerque. It cannot have escaped their notice that had the saucer not altered its flight path after being hit, it would have come down precisely there, because the distance it travelled before crashing is as near as makes no difference to the distance between where it was hit approaching Corona and Albuquerque. Those who knew the truth were well aware that if live, or probably even dead, 'aliens' fell into the wrong hands (i.e., any hands not connected to military Intelligence), it would not be long before somebody would deduce that the 'aliens' were only non-human and not extraterrestrial, and the connection between Byrd's allegedly non-existent 1947 Arctic overflight and the sudden escalation of saucer sightings in 1947 would be made, and the end of the world would ensue as surely as night follows day. At least that is what the CIA (coincidentally set up in 1947) seems to have believed and, who knows, they might have been right. From a cover-up point of view, something had to be done 'just in case' . . . but what? It had to be something that would lend itself to the disinformative strategy already in place and in use, while remaining flexible enough to leave room for future massive misdirection if a saucer and its crew should come crashing down in Central Park. Hence the ETH – the most successful secret service strategy of disinformation and misdirection in human history. And we probably owe it all to a young rock hound who excitedly gabbled on about 'Martians' in the hearing of the Intelligence operatives who were no doubt part of the army task force at the crashed saucer site.

Meanwhile, on Sunday 6 July, at the Foster Ranch outside Corona, where William 'Mac' Brazel worked as foreman, the problem of what to do about the debris he had discovered on the morning of 3 July was about to be resolved by 'Mac' Brazel taking samples of it to show to Sheriff George Willcox. The sheriff was impressed enough by Brazel's story and samples to contact nearby Roswell Army Air Force Base. I for one am certain it came as a complete surprise to the Establishment to learn that parts of the flying saucer had been lying out in the desert outside Corona for three days. However, it was a pleasant surprise, and something of a gift horse. The story of the newspaper announcement from Roswell Base telling of the finding of a flying saucer, and of the subsequent retraction and 'identification' of the debris as a 'weather balloon', is too well known to go into here at length. Can it be only coincidence that in the furore caused by the 'now we've got one . . . now we don't' announcements, the information about the site at San Agustin, where the flying saucer and crew really were, was successfully kept from the media? So effective was the cover-up about the crash site that Charles Berlitz wondered if:

Waut [the Public Information Officer at Roswell Base] might

have been ordered to leak the Roswell story to the press and write his news release specifically for the purpose of diverting attention away from the San Agustin incident.[8]

A perspicacious observation, and very probably correct, because by the time Lieutenant W.G. Haut issued his Press release, the crash retrieval at San Agustin had been under way for at least three days, so it must have been known to Colonel (later Major-General) W.H. Blanchard who authorized the release. It said that what had been found on the Foster property was not a flying saucer because that was being clandestinely retrieved from San Agustin. When the 'Roswell Statement' says, 'The flying object landed on a ranch near Roswell sometime last week. Not having phone facilities the rancher stored the disc',[9] implying that an entire saucer had been found near Roswell, it was being economical with the truth. Like much else generated by the needs of the cover-up, including the ETH, the 'Roswell Statement' was a masterpiece of misdirection, an integral part of an ongoing – although I hope to demonstrate well-meaning – disinformative agenda designed to preserve humankind from the shock of its life.

It is noticeable from the literature that there was a change in the disinformative emphasis after 1947. Flying saucer witnesses were still subjected to ridicule and social stigmatization, but concurrent with this, investigators who had some professional expertise were encouraged to waste their investigative endeavours on trying to produce evidence to force the Establishment to admit UFOs were spaceships. For over 40 years the Establishment has controlled all relevant UFO-orientated information. Despite the Freedom of Information Act, by judiciously releasing disinformation to generate a continuous ufological expectation of an ever imminent Establishment admission of an ET cover-up, it has kept ufologists chasing a cosmological chimera. By carefully orchestrating the ET 'controversy' the Establishment has directed attention away from the fact that neither the disbeliever's debunkery nor the believer's uncritical acceptance has in any way clarified the essential mystery of the UFOs, and that the study is no nearer a solution now than it was in 1947. Because of this, it is a safe bet that the Establishment's overt ufological intransigence is an argumentative ploy devised to divert attention away from the correlation that it does not wish made: that the sudden escalation of UFO sightings in 1947 was triggered by Admiral Byrd's intrusive Polar expedition, and not by aliens finding the feeble flashes of our atomic weapons in 1945 an irresistible invitation to pay us a visit.

It is unfortunate that the deeper one delves into ufology's past, the more one is made aware of weaknesses in the arguments that underpin the ETH, so that, eventually, reluctantly, you are forced to agree with Allen J. Hynek's observation, 'The man on the street's simple opinion that either UFOs are all nonsense or that visitors from outer space do exist is brutally destroyed by close study.'[10] This then leaves you with the problem of explaining why, from the documented testimony contained in the thousands of percipients' reports, investigative expertise has only resulted in the never-ending 'ET or not ET' controversy that cannot advance the argument beyond seeking to 'prove' publicly that the Establishment is concealing the ET truth by intransigently implying that there is no flying saucer mystery to investigate any way. Perhaps some indication of the accuracy of that accusation can be found in the ongoing 'non-event' scenario of 1947. In February 1947 came the North Polar overflight that never happened; then in July 1947 came the saucer crash that never happened; and finally in September 1947 came 'Majestic 12', the Intelligence operation that never happened. All these 'non-events' seem unconnected – unless you are aware of Lloyd V. Berkner's singularly synchronous ufological career, which the Establishment would like you to think also did not happen.

According to his curriculum vitae, as published in the Condon Report, Berkner was a pillar of Establishment science. Apart from admitting he was an 'engineer' with the Byrd Antarctic expedition of 1923–30, the Condon Report goes on to point out, 'The concept of an International Geophysical Year (1957–58) – the greatest example of international scientific co-operation that has yet occurred – was his brainchild.'[11] The report also mentions that Berkner served on the CIA-instigated Scientific Advisory Panel On UFOs, the infamous Robertson Panel, of January 1953. However, the report fails to mention that he had also been a founding member of the allegedly non-existent Majestic 12 Group in September 1947, and that all these endeavours, including the Antarctic expedition and the IGY, were UFO-related. What

Charles Darwin, co-creator of the increasingly insupportable
'Theory of Evolution' as applied to the origin of the human race on
planet Earth. (*Hulton-Deutsch*)

Is this evidence that something else occupies the Moon? How else can one explain the alleged existence of the word 'DAF' in a crater, or a 'stone' that has apparently rolled uphill out of a crater? (*NASA*)

A rose by any other name? This model homunculus shows what a man's body would look like if each part grew in proportion to the area of the cortex of the brain concerned with its sensory perception. (*The Natural History Museum, London*)

Can it be only coincidence that this hypothetical being, modelled by a bona fide scientist, Dr Dale A. Russell, according to scientific principles, strongly resembles the descriptions of 'aliens' given by innumerable UFO percipients? (*Canadian Museum of Nature*)

Admiral Byrd. Is this the man whose polar explorations triggered the UFO 'invasion' of 1947? (*Popperfoto*)

Intelligent dinosaur look-alikes allegedly encountered by Whitley Streiber and numerous other less well-known abductees.

Kenneth Arnold. Did he really see 'flying saucers' over the Cascades in 1947, or was he a prime mover in the Establishment disinformation initiative that has kept the real truth about UFOs from the public at large for the past 47 years? (*Author's collection*)

Left: Barney and Betty Hill were the first documented case of alleged abduction by 'intelligent dinosaur' look-alikes. This case occurred at a time when Adamski-type 'spacebrothers' were the apparent ufological norm. (*Author's collection*)

Right: How to fool most of the people all of the time?

special knowledge did Berkner have that obviously qualified him for inclusion in two Intelligence initiatives for disinforming the public about flying saucers? Could it have something to do with the fact that he was a member of the Byrd expedition that encountered the land anomaly at the poles in 1929–30, which was probably where he first saw flying saucers in their correct context? Perhaps it would be revealing to return briefly to the crash retrieval carried out in New Mexico in July 1947 and wonder why when asking:

> How could a crew of GIs, few of whom had any experience in country as wild as this, do such a thorough job of collecting all the pieces of an unknown vehicle?[12]

Stanton Friedman and Don Berliner seemed unable to spot the obvious answer, because they go on:

> No one knew what it looked like before it broke up, and so no one could estimate how much material should be in the field. And yet all of it apparently was collected.[13]

A classic example of an unwarranted assumption getting in the way of an obvious deduction. So well has the UFO community been manipulated by the Establishment that even ufologists of the calibre of Stanton Friedman are unable to think beyond the parameters of the Establishment-imposed ETH. The reason why all the pieces of the crashed saucer were retrieved was because the GIs had been briefed by someone who did know what the saucer looked like before it crashed. His name was probably Lloyd Berkner, and he had most likely seen a flying saucer while he was an 'engineer' with Byrd. On top of which is the probability that the living 'alien' also helped, as some kind of deal had probably already been struck by the American Establishment with the inhabitants of the inner Earth. Which is why, according to the testimony of Friedman's witness, the living alien:

> acted like a cat that was around kids. It just constantly watched everybody. It looked at me several times. It seemed very uneasy, even when it had calmed down to a certain degree.[14]

Just as if it knew it should not be seen by 'civilians'. How could it know the ones who found it first were 'civilians'? How can you tell the difference between any old pooch and a purpose-trained police dog? I know it probably hurts, but for an intelligent dinosaur it is probably as easy as that.

I am sure sceptics will now be wringing their hands and shouting, 'It's only speculation!' So? I like to think of it as imaginative deduction. In any case, I think I should point out that because of Establishment economy with flying saucer truth, it is probable that *everything* about them is speculation . . . even scepticism and debunkery. However, what I hope to demonstrate now is not speculation: it is the existence of Majestic 12 as a genuine Intelligence initiative for covering up the truth about the real secret of saucery. Although my ufological colleagues will think it extremely un-British of me, I am inclined to accept the proposition that if Majestic 12 never existed, 'then another group with about the same functions almost certainly did/does'.[15]

Initially, the emergence of the Majestic 12 documentation provoked a debate, mostly based on an intellectual prejudice against the possibility of 'crash retrieval', about whether the documents were genuine, a deliberate hoax or 'disinformation' foisted on Stanton Friedman to undermine his credibility by 'exposing' his gullibility once he accepted them as genuine. Stanton Friedman (a nuclear physicist) was clever enough to work all that out for himself. However, his detractors (mostly unqualified) raised inconsequential objections, and pointed to meangingless inconsistencies, which they then 'proved' and/or 'disproved' as if it mattered. Friedman and his associates withstood the slings and arrows of outrageous ufologists and stuck to their guns. The real argumentative acumen of their detractors was finally exposed by an insinuation that the name Detlev Bronk was an obvious alias, when in fact even minimal research would have revealed that *Dr* Detlev Bronk, founder of the science of biophysics, had been one of the really big guns of American science since 1946 at least. Fortunately, that final *faux pas* seems to have been the nadir of all the quite unnecessary objections, and Friedman and his associates were left to carry on their enquiries with their customary professional dedication. However, the matter still seems not to be entirely resolved, and I would like now to draw attention to some singularly synchronous material that could, if true according to my interpretation, go all the way to corroborating the actual existence of the Majestic 12 group, or at the very least another one that served the same purpose and function. According to the allegedly suspect documentation discussed by Friedman, one particular member of the original Majestic 12 group was Secretary James V. Forrestal. Unfortunately he died and his place was not filled, according to Stanton Friedman, until 1 August 1950, when a General Walter B. Smith was designated as his permanent replacement. Coincidentally:

> Project Magnet, established in December 1950 was headed by Mr Wilbert B. Smith of the Telecommunications Division of the Canadian Department of Transport who was officially authorized by the Deputy Minister of Transport for Air Services to make as detailed a study of the UFO Phenomenon as could be accomplished within the framework of existing Canadian establishments.[16]

Apparently, this same Wilbert B. Smith, in response to a question about who was organizing the suspect ET information cover-up said: 'It was a small group very high up in the government.'[17] Then he clammed up and refused to identify the group. From another source it is possible to surmise that the group he was referring to was 'known in the innermost circle of the Eisenhower Administration as the "54/12 Group"'.[18] That this clandestine '54/12 Group' is also credited with being:

> a hitherto Classified adjunct of the National Security Council, specially charged by the President with ruling on special operations[19]

only serves to emphasize its similarity with the Majestic 12 group. So when it is claimed that the '54/12 Group'

> operated in an atmosphere of secrecy exceeding that of any other branch of the United States' Government[20]

it can be seen as conclusive confirmation that 'Majestic 12' and '54/12' were one and the same, and that this corroborative correlation practically proves the actual existence of 'Majestic 12'. And what of the close resemblance of the names Walter B. Smith and Wilbert B. Smith? The best that can be made of that at the moment is to acknowledge that this kind of name coincidence is seemingly an integral part of the mythology of ufology. If you don't believe me, ask John A. Keel, whose magnum opus *Operation Trojan Horse* drew attention to this fortean facet of flying saucery.

Taking it as proven that Friedman and Berliner are correct in their assertion that Majestic 12 was genuine, it can be understood why, as convinced and convincing proponents of the ETH, they found it difficult to comprehend the inclusion of Donald Menzel in the group and asked, 'Was his inclusion in the MJ-12 Group a slip up on the part of some unknown and possibly playful hoaxer?'[21] Even though they had earlier answered their own question by pointing out that Donald Menzel was, at that time, 'best known for three books in which he ridiculed UFOs and those who took them seriously'.[22] A point emphasized by Menzel's dismissal of Clyde Tombaugh's Flying Saucer report in a way 'that made it appear that Tombaugh [the discoverer of the Planet Pluto] was unable to tell his azimuth form his elevation'.[23] Seen in this light, Menzel's inclusion in the Majestic 12 group is quite understandable. The real 'mystery' candidate has to be Lloyd V. Berkner. All the other members, including Menzel, had either strong Intelligence or military affiliations. Compared to the rest of his Majestic 12 colleagues, Lloyd Berkner was, at that time, apparently underqualified to be included among such a group of VIPs. Yet, even then, he must have had hidden talents, because of all the members of Majestic 12 only he went on to be included in the Scientific Advisory Panel on UFOs in 1953:

> Known in UFO legend as 'The Robertson Panel' – which apparently was the first major CIA funded attempt to 'debunk' UFOs in such a way as to persaude the general public that the subject was only fit for discussion by the demented.[24]

Then he was instrumental in the staging of the International Geophysical Year (IGY) of 1957–58 which many at the time alleged was a cover-up for a global scientific UFO search, and which saw, especially in the Antarctic, the beginning of a curious co-operation between the superpowers. Can it be only coincidence that the IGY began only a year after Byrd, returning from 'the most important expedition in the history of the world', had announced in March 1956 that 'the present expedition has opened up a vast new territory'?[25] As one of those who knew precisely what Admiral Byrd was referring to, and who had probably known since being with him on his Antarctic expedition of 1929–30, who was better qualified than Lloyd V. Berkner to be included in the Majestic 12 group? This was the élite group that was formed in 1947, at the behest of President Truman, to keep secret the survival of a superior intelligent dinosaur race inside the planet we thought was ours.

Almost certainly, 1947 was pivotal in shaping future flying saucery, and the reason for this is what Lloyd V. Berkner told his Majestic 12 colleagues.

References

[1] *The Hollow Earth*, Dr Raymond Bernard (Carol Paperbacks, 1991).
[2] *Scientific Study of UFOs* (Condon Report), introduction by Walter Sullivan (Bantam Extra, 1969).
[3] *Flying Saucers on the Attack*, Harold Wilkins (Ace, 1967).
[4] *The Roswell Incident*, Charles Berlitz and William Moore (Granada, 1980).
[5] ibid.
[6] *Crash at Corona*, Stanton T. Friedman and Don Berliner (Paragon House, 1992).
[7] ibid.
[8] Berlitz and Moore, op. cit.
[9] ibid.
[10] *UFOs – The Final Answer?*, ed. David Barclay and Therese Maria Barclay (Blandford, 1993).
[11] Condon Report, op. cit.
[12] Friedman and Berliner, op. cit.
[13] ibid.
[14] ibid.
[15] ibid.
[16] Condon Report, op. cit.
[17] Bernard, op. cit.
[18] ibid.
[19] ibid.
[20] ibid.
[21] ibid.
[22] Friedman and Berliner, op. cit.
[23] Barclay, op. cit.
[24] 'Majestic 12 – Disinformation or Dreadful Truth?', Philip Asher, *The UFO Debate*, No. 2.
[25] Bernard, op. cit.

CHAPTER 7

The EBE Jeebies

CONSIDERING the very real possibility that they could turn out to be the dominant life form on this planet, the creatures who career around in flying saucers have had a pretty raw deal from ufologists. Initially ignored, or disparaged as the LGM (little green men) from Mars, they were relegated to the realms of those individuals whom the serious scientific ufologists designated 'the lunatic fringe'. This inevitably meant that the nascent ufological investigative initiative was unbalanced, because the emphasis was only on reports of things seen in the sky, especially those that described 'structured craft', since these were the ones most amenable to the favoured explanation of 'spaceship'. The early investigators obviously felt more secure with reports of daylight discs or meandering nocturnal lights, because the investigation of these – it was fondly hoped – would lend itself to the 'scientific method' as conceived by ufologists and any reports containing references to 'flying saucer occupants' were viewed with deep distrust. For this initial – and in some quarters still influential – attitude, a 'civilian' UFO society must take most of the blame. Despite the fact that there were other civilian UFO investigation groupings around at the time, the National Investigations Committee for Aerial Phenomena (NICAP) seemed to dominate the field. It was probably through the influence of this one group that a kind of ersatz military/scientific jargon came to pervade ufology, and ufologists' awful addiction to acronyms took permanent hold. It seemed, in those far gone days, that those interested in flying saucers had decided that, in order to impress their detractors, the military/scientific Establishment, they must become poor imitations of them. Ufologists began to write and speak like the actors in *Earth Vs the Flying Saucers*, which had been 'based' on the allegedly non-fiction book *Flying Saucers From Outer Space* by none other than the Director of NICAP, Donald E. Keyhoe, a 'retired' Marine Corps major. Almost single-handedly, beginning in January 1950 with his article 'Flying Saucers Are Real' in *True* magazine, and then through his books and NICAP, he proclaimed, and without a shred of real evidence, promoted the view that 'for the past 175 years, the planet Earth has been under systematic close range examination by living, intelligent observers from another planet.'[1] From there he went on to advance obsessively the accusation that the scientific/military Establishment was conducting a cover-up to keep that ET 'truth' from the general public. As with Kenneth Arnold, it has to be suspected that Major Keyhoe spoke with a forked tongue and that his apparent dedication to the cause of exposing the ET truth was just another Establishment-orchestrated piece of misdirection. That there was something suspect about Keyhoe's allegedly anti-Establishment UFO society is maintained by the fact that, after he became director, it seemed to attract a remarkable number of 'ex' Establishment types to its membership – of whom Major Dewey J. Fournet, former Pentagon monitor of the Air Force UFO Project, Sign, is an excellent example. The society also never really experienced any trouble in obtaining the kind of information that practically proved that flying saucers existed and were interplanetary machines. In those halcyon days, under the direction of Keyhoe, NICAP seemingly became the best ETH-inclined UFO rumour machine in the world. However, the *coup de grâce* to Keyhoe's credibility comes with the realization that he had a close connection with Admiral Richard E. Byrd, and in fact 'managed Adm. Byrd's North Pole [isn't that the expedition that never happened?] plane tour of the U.S'.[2] This link adequately explains why he was probably chosen by the Establishment to help them create and maintain the diversionary ETH mythology. I say 'probably chosen' because it is equally possible that, knowing what Byrd discovered at the North Pole and what it meant, he volunteered. It is also feasible to suppose that he knew Lloyd Berkner, who also had Navy affiliations. In fact, it might be germane to this issue to mention here that the Marine Corps seems to have had a closer association with the UFO phenomenon than either the army or the air force, so much so that one is led to wonder if the air force involvement was just another ploy in the overall strategy of misdirection of the masses. The dichotomy of the antipathy on Keyhoe's part, and hence NICAP's, towards reports of LGM, UFO occupants, etc. while trumpeting the truth of the ETH is easily explained by remembering what both he and his hidden masters in the Establishment were really trying to cover up. Misdirection is the name of the game the Establishment continuously plays in its ongoing attempt to put off the awful day when the probability that the creatures who bred the human race as a bio-servomechanism – and, presumably could prove it – are alive and well and living in Shangri-La, Belovodye, Schamballah, Agharti, or whatever name you want to give to the 'hidden kingdom' allegedly inside the Earth, becomes public knowledge.

Reading through the massive amount of documentation in the literature dealing with the UFO phenomenon, one is made acutely aware that the one facet of the mystery that causes the most difficulty to those who would explain what is happening is the reported behaviour of alleged UFO occupants. Time and again in reports these extraterrestrial creatures behave as if they were at home on planet Earth. In many ways, it is a pity that ufology got sidetracked by the contactee claims of Adamski, Menger and their imitators, because even today, it is unclear if they were the hoaxers or if they were the hoaxed. The problem is that they present ufology as a whole:

> By mixing a certain amount of the real thing with a certain amount of sensational nonsense, then presenting it scrambled up together to be accepted or rejected as a whole, it is possible to make unfamiliar subject matter seem repugnant and unfit for study by intelligent people, while attracting the ignorant like flies.[3]

In the case of George Adamski, the original and best purveyor of the interplanetary spacebrother scenario, it can be argued that almost single-handedly he scuppered any hope that the subject of flying saucer occupants might get serious scientific attention by using what seems to have been the *modus operandi* detailed in the above quote. This observation makes possible the inevitable deduction that:

> It is entirely possible that he may have been a CIA disinformation agent, who successfully fulfilled the mission of

making the subject of UFOs seem so absurd that no independent in-depth investigation would be made by qualified academics.[4]

A contributory clue to who Adamski's flying saucer friends really were is that:

People who travelled with Adamski noticed that he had been issued a special passport, such as is reserved for diplomats and high government officials.[5]

In spite of this, and to be fair, it has to be considered possible that at least some of the more trusting souls who espoused alien contact did in fact interact with someone/thing that purported to be from Mars, Venus and even Uranus. Yet so strong is the embarrassment factor inherent in contacteeism that it cannot be beyond the bounds of probability that the whole thing was part and parcel of the Establishment's diversionary designs. What better way to frighten off the sensible than to encourage cosmological cultists and conmen publicly to pursue their interplanetary excesses? In this context, it is as well to remember that one of the complaints levelled against Edward U. Condon, the Director of the ill-fated Colorado Project (1966–69), was that he apparently gave more attention to the way-out spacebrother stories of the cosmologically creative than he did to the more sober business of the scientific study of UFOs he was supposed to be leading at the University of Colorado. However, in his defence, it must be remembered that the Colorado Project, as with all Establishment-sponsored investigative initiatives, probably had a covert agenda that was diametrically opposed to the overt public one. Therefore, it is more than likely that Condon was only doing what was expected of him.

Without being dogmatic one way or the other, it has to be said that it probably came as something of a relief to ufology when all those aliens with names like the latest acrylic fibres began to evaporate from the investigative scene. But the relief was to be short lived as reports describing the kind of UFO-related creatures who eventually came to be known as EBEs (extra-terrestrial biological entities) started to proliferate. This seeming upsurge in entity activity was something of a ufoloptical illusion, because the kind of experiences that involved creatures less spacebrotherly and more non-human had been occurring since the very early days. It was just that the reports concerning them had been ignored, possibly because of a misplaced sense of ufological propriety – a perfectly understandable attitude when it is realized that before the Hills' abduction was publicized in 1966:

> On the other hand, UFO researchers had been confronted with the religious machinations of the 'contactee cult' which claimed communication and contact with friendly 'space brothers' (not unlike angels in their apparent intentions and appearance).
> On the other, there were the often too frequent accounts of unexplainable small hairy bipeds, small humanoids with oversized heads and nearly average human-sized manlike beings.[6]

One writer who was not afraid to address the subject of diminutive UFO occupants was Frank Scully, who wrote *Behind the Flying Saucers*, published in 1950. At the time, Scully's book was thoroughly 'debunked' (which I hasten to add is *not* the same as refuted) and he himself was socially stigmatized, but:

> Although generally rejected by most researchers in the early years, subsequent incidents seem to indicate that Scully was either telling the truth or that he was a prophet.[7]

As reports of UFO occupants increased in quantity, if not in quality, it became clear that a growing number of witnesses seemed to be describing the kind of entity referred to by Scully. Equally indicative that Scully's book had been closer to the mark than many of his colleagues admitted was a statement allegedly made to Scully and his wife by Edward Ruppelt in 1953. Then no longer head of Project Blue Book, Ruppelt apparently felt able to tell Scully, 'Confidentially, of all the books that have been published about flying saucers, your book was the one that gave us the most headaches because it was closest to the truth.'[8] When this alleged admission was made, the almost unavoidable insecurities characterizing ufological investigations of this kind were sufficiently strong to make the investigators speculate that, because of the apparently enervating effect of the Scully book on UFO occupant research, perhaps 'the authorities concerned with the cover-up might even have encouraged the publication of

Behind the Flying Saucers as a subterfuge aiding to discredit the initial reports.'[9]

While on the subject of Captain Ruppelt and the possibility that Scully was part of some fiendishly clever Establishment disinformative exercise, I would like to ask: who invented the designation Unidentified Flying Object (UFO) and, perhaps more importantly, why? The answer would seem to be that:

> The elaboration [flying saucer] on Arnold's allusion to a 'saucer' was employed almost exclusively until Captain Ruppelt was assigned to direct Project Blue Book, the small United States Air Force unit responsible for monitoring, investigating, and evaluating the aerial phenomena. He coined the phrase 'Unidentified Flying Object' (frequently acronymically condensed to U-F-O, or, less often 'you-foe') to distinguish what appeared to be rational sighting reports from ones sounding like excerpts from fairy-tales or nightmares.[10]

I would suggest that it is far more probable that the term Unidentified Flying Object (UFO, OOFO or You-Foe) was introduced by Ruppelt because it allowed reports about almost anything (meteors, satellites, seagulls, the Moon, aeroplanes and even dustbin liners) that underinformed and over-excitable witnesses could not immediately 'identify' to be submitted for 'study'. This, while giving Blue Book the opportunity to obtain a steady supply of 'sightings' that could be explained as misperceptions of mundane phenomena, would also allow the real paucity of Blue Book's investigative efforts to be hidden behind statistics (that mostly never added up anyway) that included them. What has to be kept in mind always is that initially what was reported were *not* Unidentified Flying Objects, but rather Objects (i.e., flying saucers) that had been identified by the percipient as being unlike anything resembling a conventional plane. Introducing the notion of Unidentified Flying Objects, embodying as it does an unwarranted assumption, aided the Establishment in opening the floodgates to the kind of report that would help them effectively to lose the flying saucer 'signal' in among the UFO 'noise'. At the same time it gave the impression of trying to conduct an impartial and informed investigation against all the odds and an incoming tide of tedious misidentifications. As we all know, the ploy worked and, even today, people readily report UFOs – usually anything they cannot identify personally, which, where the general public is concerned, can be quite a lot. If the same rationale is applied to the, as yet unproven, identification of flying saucer occupants as Extraterrestrial Biological Entities, it would mean that the classification EBE could be to flying saucer occupants what Unidentified Flying Object (UFO) is to their vehicles: an unwarranted assumption that assists the Establishment in maintaining the misdirection that has kept the investigation of flying saucers going in circles for over 40 years.

Perhaps *the* major obstacle preventing a sensible solution to the problem of flying saucer occupants is the fact that so many different types have been reported. Even taking into account the probability of disinformation by the Establishment, and fabrication of reports by sundry notoriety seekers, or hoaxes by others with different disinformative axes to grind, this apparent multiplicity of occupant types is still something that many ufologists have difficulty in coming to terms with in any context other than that of the ETH. In this respect, the one aspect of human-alien interactions most glossed over, or even ignored entirely, is the fact that flying saucer occupants are regularly reported as not wearing a 'space helmet'. This would seem to indicate that, wherever it is they are allegedly from, they are able to breathe our atmosphere like natives. That would not be so bad if only one particularly 'humanoid' type did it, because it could be argued that it was statistically possible that at least one other planet could have produced life in an oxygen-based atmosphere. But when the non-oxygen breathers – that is, those occupants who are reported as wearing breathing apparatus or a space helmet – seem to be a vanishing minority, as the ufological record apparently shows them to be, then either something is wrong with science's beliefs about the Universe, or something is wrong with ufologists' beliefs about EBEs. Or, perhaps as with much else in ufology, it could be just another example of an Establishment-imposed unwarranted assumption getting in the way of what should be an obvious deduction. Surely, if flying saucer opponents seem able to breathe our atmosphere, tolerate our gravity and generally behave like us, the answer to where they come from is obvious: planet Earth, of course. This devastating deduction is in part confirmed by Gordon Creighton's observation of the fact that 'there is much evidence that *some* of what we nowadays call "beings from flying saucers" are much more probably creatures who share this Earth with us'.[11] Only some? I hardly think so.

The change in the alien intrusion format from Adamski's long-haired Venusians to the less well-favoured intelligent dinosaur lookalikes is thought to have occurred at the time the Barney and Betty Hill abduction episode was made public in John Fuller's *Interrupted Journey*, published *circa* 1966 – although the incident it exhaustively examines had occurred years earlier, on the night of 19 September 1961. Certainly, the Hills' experience embodied much that was to become *de rigueur* in later abduction scenarios, but there was one abduction that predated theirs which contained the one abductive element against which all others would eventually pale into insignificance. The abduction was that of Antonio Villas Boas in South America on the night of 5 October 1957, and the element was the possibility of flying saucer occupant hybridization experiments. In ufology, as in everything else, sex had finally reared its head and nothing was going to be the same again. No wonder Orthon and Firkon and other similar spacebrothers went away for good; they were probably just too embarrassed to hang around. Spacebrotherly love is one thing, but sex is something else again. As with all the cases that time has turned into classics, the interpretation of the Villas Boas abduction, has ossified around the assumptions of the ETH. But there is an alternative, and I don't mean the one that implies Villas Boas was a suitable case for treatment. I am sure the parameters of the Villas Boas abduction are too well known to need reiteration here. In any case, it is only the sexual element that needs to be readdressed in order to indicate that when the case was first 'analysed' an ET solution was reached by some Olympic-standard conclusion jumping. From Boas's narrative, it is clear that he was already thinking in terms of space aliens when he gave his testimony to Dr Olavo Fontes. It is equally clear from this testimony that the flying saucer occupants he interacted with were no more alien to Earth than he was. The female he described was obviously 'humanoid' enough to cause a strong sexual arousal in Villas Boas by virtue of her nakedness. Although he tried to imply that he mated with her almost against his will, it is a fact, derived from his own testimony, that – forced or not – he had intercourse with her twice, and would have tried for the hat trick had she not refused him. But what has that got to do with where she came from? The fact that they engaged in intercourse speaks volumes. Any racially non-related, 'space alien', humanoid female exchanging body fluids with an Earth man is inevitably committing suicide, with murder on the side. We humans contain organisms which would kill us if we did not have immune systems, specifically developed over the millennia, to prevent them. Therefore, a lady from space would stand no chance, because her immune system would have been developed to defend her against the murderous micro-organisms of her own world, so it would provide no protection against terrestrial micro-organisms – a state of affairs which also applies to an Earth-based immune system when and if confronted by non-Earth organisms. Any member of a superior interstellar civilization must have known this and would have made Villas Boas wear a condom, at the very least. In addition to this, any alleged superior interstellar civilization would have known that members of two distinct races – and you cannot get more distinct than being from different worlds – cannot produce viable offspring because their chromosome counts do not match. So, for the Villas Boas-flying saucer occupant intercourse to produce viable progeny – which by her gestures at the end of the experience his alien partner clearly conveyed that she expected it would – the pair of them must have been racially related. Taking into account also that Villas Boas did not subsequently succumb to any infection, this would only be possible if both were from Earth – and shared something else that will be touched on later.

A further indication that Villas Boas's abductors were Earth-based is the fact that these allegedly alien entities – in particular the female – breathed our atmosphere with apparent impunity (the argument about lethal micro-organisms applies to the atmosphere too, so it isn't just a matter of them being oxygen breathers from a planet similar to Earth). Olavo Fontes, obviously only thinking in terms of the ETH, commented:

> I could not understand how the crew could breathe, being fastened into those clothes and wearing those helmets all the time, with no portable reserves in sight. [12]

Villas Boas, while quite truthful, answered from the standpoint of one who had already made the unwarranted assumption of extraterrestriality on the part of his abductors, because he said:

> I hadn't thought of it in fact. I cannot explain it either. I didn't
> notice anything at all, no bulge or lump to show the tubes were
> fastened somewhere to a box or contrivance hidden under their
> clothes.[13]

Of course there was no bulge to indicate breathing apparatus:
there was no breathing apparatus. Like you and me, Villas Boas's
abductors apparently did not need any, and probably for the same
reason that we do not.

It is noticeable how, since the seminal abductions of Villas Boas
and Barney and Betty Hill, the abduction experience has
overtaken and largely replaced the earlier contactee syndrome.
The early altruism of the so-called Nordic-type flying saucer
occupants has been replaced by an insensitive intrusiveness on
the part of creatures who have apparently come to resemble more
and more the 'hypothetical intelligent dinosaur' modelled by Dr
Dale Russell. This almost hostile behaviour by flying saucer
occupants is not something that has suddenly appeared in more
recent reports, it is something that has been endemic, if
unadmitted, in reports dating back to the earliest days. This
hostility is difficult to accommodate in the ETH simply because if
UFOs had represented an invasion of earth by a superior
interstellar civilization, it would have been all over bar the
shouting by this time. It must stand to reason that any extraterrestrial civilization considering conquest, and with a technology
to get them here, would inevitably have had a technology so
advanced that they would have just walked in and taken charge.
But they didn't, they haven't, and they show no signs of doing so.
Therefore, it seems likely that something other than interplanetary
invasion is going on. But what?

The most disturbing development in the whole flying saucer
occupant scenario is not the fact that these creatures have been
inaccurately identified as EBE, but the ever-expanding sexual
abuse scenario which has them conducting intimate experiments,
allegedly resulting in offspring which are a cross between human
and alien. The EBE advocates see this experimentation as a
strategy on the part of the aliens to improve their stock,
something that Villas Boas also speculated. This particular plot is

the biological equivalent of the one that had the invaders trying to find a replacement planet for their own which was in some kind of terminal situation. A moment's thought will put such a hybridization possibility beyond the pale, because it is about as sensible as humans cross-breeding with gorillas to improve our racial stock. Apart from the fact it would not work, because of the difference in human and gorilla chromosome counts, it is illogical to suppose an improvement can be obtained by mating with an evolutionary inferior. Yet, there now seems no doubt that the flying saucer occupants are engaged in an initiative to produce, or at least lead sundry persons to believe they are producing, alien–human children. Why they should be doing this, I cannot say – yet. However, it is an occupant strategy that goes back a lot further than those presently engaged in the investigation of the phenomenon might realize. Indeed, as far back as 1967, when Brad Steiger and Joan Whritenour wrote that they had 'on file':

> the claim of a young California woman that she was raped by an occupant of an UFO. There is also a deposition by her doctor who testifies to having treated the young woman for a premature delivery of a stillborn baby that seemed to have been the product of highly dubious mixed breeding.[14]

A claim such as that might have been considered ufologically outrageous *circa* 1967, but sadly similar claims have since become commonplace. All the ramifications inherent in this 'reproductive' facet of flying saucer occupant operations have not yet been properly addressed, nor will they be until investigators can disabuse themselves of the idea that a totally unrelated alien life form, from a planet other than Earth, is producing a hybrid of itself and *Homo sapiens*. Even if it could do such a thing, why would it want to? Isn't it being just a mite over-anthropocentric to presume that superior cosmic beings have nothing better to occupy their time than to travel light years in order to dilute/pollute their racial gene pool with that of an inferior species? In speculating about the 'greys', who seem to be central to abduction/impregnation claims, Bud Hopkins makes the usual unproven allegation about EBEs when he attempts to argue that 'whatever the nature and the origins of the grey-skinned UFO occupants – and there are many exotic theories – they are not us'.[15] Unfortunately, this might turn out to be just another of those unwarranted ufological assumptions, because the evidence he has unearthed (impregnation and even a period of gestation producing a baby) argues the opposite. For pregnancy to occur, whatever life form donated the sperm, it must have had an unsuspected genetic interface with the human race. It cannot be claimed that successful impregnation is due to the greys employing an ill-defined 'superior' genetic/medical procedure, because it is demonstrable from the data that this strange breeding programme is being facilitated using both male and female abductees. According to Bud Hopkins:

> Over the past six years [1980–86] I have worked with four male abductees who have described encounters very similar to Villas Boas's abduction, and three others whose incomplete accounts strongly suggest such an event.[16]

From such detail there seems little doubt that 'breeding' experiments have been going on since 1957. The only problem now seems to be making some sense of them. It's just too easy a get out to say of the greys:

> They are alien. And as such their purposes and goals – even their mental processes – are possibly unknowable by us humans.[17]

when all the evidence points unerringly to the opposite conclusion – even if it is a conclusion that seems unlikely to conform to the requirements of human chauvinism. Biological these entities demonstrably are, but their extraterrestriality is open to question.

References

[1] 'Flying Saucers Are Real', Donald E. Keyhoe, The *True* Report on Flying Saucers (Fawcett, 1967).
[2] ibid.
[3] *Extra-Terrestrials Among Us*, George C. Andrews (Llewellyn Publications, 1992).
[4] ibid.
[5] ibid.
[6] *Flying Saucer Occupants*, Coral and Jim Lorenzen (Signet, 1967).

[7] ibid.

[8] *The Roswell Incident*, Charles Berlitz and William Moore (Granada, 1980).

[9] ibid.

[10] *UFO Exist!*, Paris Flammonde (Ballantine, 1977).

[11] *The Humanoids*, ed. Charles Bowen (Neville Spearman, 1969).

[12] Lorenzen, op. cit.

[13] ibid.

[14] *Flying Saucers Are Hostile*, Brad Steiger and Joan Whritenour (Award/Tandem, 1967).

[15] *Intruders*, Bud Hopkins (Sphere, 1988).

[16] ibid.

[17] ibid.

CHAPTER 8
Ye Gods?

THERE is an aspect peculiar to ufology that makes it unique. Despite having pretentions to being a purely secular science attempting to determine whether or not spaceships with extra-terrestrials are whizzing around in our atmosphere, ufology has developed an ancillary explanatory option with religious over-tones. Ostensibly, this accounts for the incongrous 'psychic' element within what otherwise, it would like to insist, is an objectively real phenomenon. Such is the present influence of this psychic/spiritual aspect of ufology that Whitley Streiber, a recent abductee/contactee, can confidently claim, 'The only thing now needed to make the UFO myth a new religion of remarkable scope and force is a single undeniable sighting.'[1] Ludicrous as it might seem to those who subscribe solely to the Extraterrestrial Hypothesis (ETH), there is a connection between UFO manifes-tations and religious experiences, and it has very little to do with the percipients but – amazingly – a lot to do with the phenomenon itself. It is almost as if whatever operates as the UFO phenomenon wants to be identified with spirituality rather than mere secular space travel, purveying to its percipients a kind of 'philosophy', that has the Almighty and aliens co-operating in the 'salvation' of the human race from indeterminate cosmic catastrophes. It is all very New Age and mostly nonsensical, and sometimes it borders on the blasphemous. Yet there is no denying the allure of this aspect of ufology since it has adherents throughout the worldwide UFO community.

It would not be such a problem if it could be shown that the spiritual side of ufology was the result of purely human misinterpretation of the ufological experience. Unfortunately, quite the opposite is obvious, with the manifesting intelligence apparently going out of its way to inject an unequivocal spiritual element into what otherwise could have been easily interpreted as a confrontation with an ET. So it is that the contactee syndrome, abduction experience, entity enigma – call it what you will – has become the worm in the apple of scientific ufology. Just when it had begun to look possible for the conservative core of ufologists to accept the existence of Extraterrestrial Biological Entities (EBEs) as the culprits responsible for the abduction of, and exobiological experimentation upon, sundry members of the human race, they were confronted with evidence indicating a scientifically unacceptable spiritual dimension to initially secular 'spacenappings'.

In the days before the advance of human technology, and the even quicker advance of pulp science fiction magazines, made possible public speculation about space travel and the invasion of Earth by aliens, the various, more or less humanoid 'apparitions' were seen as the sole property of either religion or occultism – sometimes both. These two belief systems, each with their sectarian and often superstitious spin offs, were equal to the task of explaining the entity experience in terms of the prevailing pre-scientific cultural paradigm. Ghosts, angels, demons, hidden chiefs, ascended adeptii, saints, Satan and, especially, the Blessed Virgin Mary (BVM) played their part in preserving the prerogatives of the various competing 'tunnel realities'. Even when spiritualism came along, the paranormal paradigm was flexible enough to accommodate 'Summerland' within its boundaries, and to add to the list of astral entities the spiritualistically obligatory Native American Indian guide and others of the same ilk as they came along. The various paranormal personages kept within the boundaries of the belief systems supporting them, and everything worked wonderfully . . . until the flying saucers flew in. Now, Monka from Mars Sector Seven, who began 'communicating' through the mediumship of George King, founder of the Etherius society, has seemingly been promoted to:

Head of the Presidium for our Solar Government which meets on Saturn. He now has responsibilities with our Galaxies of Planets and has been given the title 'Protector of our Planet Earth'.[2]

and now espouses a kind of Blavatskian blarney while claiming to be, at one and the same time:

> your space brother, the protector of planet Earth, and an Ascended Master[3]

which is kind of gilding the lily a little, don't you think? No more so than Jesus who, under his cosmic name of Sananda, allegedly attends the interplanetary parliament on Uranus, and apparently now rejects the more orthodox accounts of his Earthly ministry in favour of an occult version called 'The Aquarian Gospel of Jesus Christ' by Eliphas Levi, a sometime 'magician' and probable diabolist. Any number of alleged space beings now spout spiritualistic 'philosophy', as channelled by their various 'mediums' (i.e. contactees), and they are apparently queueing up to pontificate the kind of meaningless metaphysics that used to be the sole property of the discarnate divines from Summerland. I hope they are not infringing copyright. It is so easy to mock the beliefs of those who perhaps see in flying saucery a means to enhance and make more meaningful their often mundane lives. Because of this, we have to ask: why do allegedly intelligent and 'superior' aliens always seem to pick on the nondescript through which to channel their messages of 'supreme cosmic importance'? The sensible answer would seem to be that there are no space-brothers and it is all down to self-delusion on the part of the otherwise ineffectual. On the other hand, it could be confidence trickery on the part of those who prosper by combining the 'cosmic wisdom' about there being one born every minute with the 'higher truth' that says a fool and his money are soon parted, except that there is evidence to indicate that such a sensible solution is probably as far from the real truth as you can get.

If it were only a matter of dealing with the kind of cosmology bequeathed to ufology by the likes of George Adamski, then the task of sifting the chaff from the wheat would be a simple task indeed. Unfortunately, there is evidence to suggest that George wasn't actually lying, but only passing on what he had been told by entities purporting to be solar spacefarers. If so, we can only wonder, in view of Adamski's probable connection with the American Establishment, who was hoaxing whom about what and to what eventual purpose? There is an answer, of course, and quite a simple one, providing you lay aside all unwarranted assumptions regarding the meaning of life. It is, perhaps, a little early to embark on an explanation of that statement, but part of the answer is in the saucerian significance of the book *OAHSPE*, published in 1882, the contents of which leaves no doubt that 'the gods and their legions of angels are flying around the universe in circular, disclike ships'.[4] This book was allegedly dictated by angels to a New York dentist. What can angels be up to dealing in space travel? What next I wonder? Would you believe a book about Atlantis that describes a form of transport called a vailx?

> A drawing or painting of the vailx is included in the book. The similarity between the vailx and the flying saucers seen in the 1950s, particularly that 'photographed' by contactee George Adamski (1955), is truly remarkable.[5]

Perhaps even more remarkable was the title of this book, published in 1894, which, while ostensibly about Atlantis, was called *A Dweller on Two Planets*.

Skyscrapers of speculation could be built upon so-called 'mythological' material, similar to the above, which has ostensibly spiritual beings implying some connection with extraterrestrials. Emmanuel Swedenborg (1688–1772) claimed that extraterrestrial entities astrally 'abducted' him in April 1744, via an out of the body experience (OOBE), to see 'Heaven' and 'Hell'. During the trip he met 'Jesus'. Surely such composite cosmologies were only possible in Swedenborg's day because the realities of space flight were a mystery. Surely nobody these days would, or could, think of using OOBE as a means to space travel? Especially not allegedly objectively real EBEs. You think not?

In October 1952 Cecil Michael saw a 'Flying Saucer'. It was an experience that left him in no doubt that 'aliens' were visiting Earth. A few days later, on the morning of 14 October, two human-looking individuals turned up at his workshop. But, although Michael says of them that:

> They were really nice looking men, just as natural and solid looking as any human being could look.[6]

it is obvious that he accepted them as the beings whose saucer he had seen only a few days previously. However, even during the early stages of his experience, these ostensibly extraterrestrial beings displayed talents that can only be considered as being paranormal. They could render themselves invisible at will, and conversed telepathically. Eventually, Michael claims, they 'abducted' him. That the adventure was 'astral' from the outset is clear from the victim's narrative. What is interesting to me about it is that he was taken by them to the planet 'Hell', where he met the Devil, saw the damned being hurled into a lake of fire, and was eventually rescued by Jesus – a definite 'Swedenborgian' scenario. The experience, especially the part relating to the abduction, was in large measure 'unreal'. This is unequivocally indicated by the victim's constant references to being 'jerked back' to his workshop throughout the entire abduction experience, ostensibly to attend to mundane business matters, like answering the phone or serving customers. After completion of these tasks, he was forcibly returned to the abduction scenario at the point where it had been interrupted. That the witness himself was aware of this strange bilocation of his consciousness is attested to by his comment, 'What I experienced did not interfere with me in my work or my business in any way.'[7] This would seem to indicate that some part of the percipient was taken rampaging around the universe while his body stayed *in situ* on some kind of autopilot. This situation, while obviously confusing to Mr Michael, does have its parallels in the literature of OOBE and even in documented UFO abductions. In fact, this cross-fertilization between the so-called psychic and the scientific is one of the most disturbing facets of ufology. In the case of Cecil Michael, it resulted in a narrative that was peripherally technological when dealing with the sighting of the UFO and in the details of the subsequent space flight to planet Hell. If the percipient's recollections of the experience had gone straight from sighting to abduction and interplanetary journey, without touching on the strange workshop segment, it is highly likely that ufologists would have had another classic abduction to analyse and another ET witness to patronize. But there is the workshop segment, and that the witness who, by his own admission, was aware of there being 'two of him', a condition about which he asked his abductors, but got no reply. Because of the way the experience evolved, it has to be considered as possible, perhaps even probable, that everything after the initial sighting was an hypnogogic adventure of some kind. Too bad virtual reality technology wasn't around in 1952 to suggest a scientific solution to these experiences, because a so-called 'altered state of consciousness' has come to characterize the entity experience as a whole, even when EBE lookalikes are involved.

Seen from this paranormal perspective, it is little wonder that science has signally failed to confront the UFO enigma. In the entity experience was the potential for science to become impaled as never before on the Sword of the Spirit that it had for so long tried to beat into an atheistic ploughshare. It was bad enough that people continued to report seeing apparently alien aeroforms when Establishment science had done its best to exorcise them, but it was infinitely worse when in among the technological trappings associated with EBE 'abductions' there began to appear, with increasing frequency, elements undeniably occult or religious. To compound even 'scientific' ufological consternation at this turn of events, the investigators were convinced that theosophical and theological elements were being deliberately introduced into the overall abduction experience by the entities. At least one staunch supporter of the ETH, in reference to unexpected theological material in an abduction he was investigating, anxiously agonized in print, 'We dare not dismiss it, because it may provide the focal point, the very reason, for the abduction.'[8] The investigator was Raymond Fowler and the abduction he was investigating was Betty Andreasson's. At first satisfyingly scientific, the alleged encounter with seeming EBEs subsequently provided details, obtained under hypnosis, that caused Fowler to write 'a religious connotation caused great consternation among us'.[9] In its own way, that remark is one of the classic understatements in ufology. Betty Andreasson's religious vision ended forever any idea that UFO entities were alien to this planet. Whatever they are, in the Andreasson abduction they displayed their familiarity with human religious metaphor, their ability to imply convincingly deity, and their complete command of the 'phantasmagoric' reality into which they networked their victim. Ham-strung by their unwarranted ETH assumptions, Fowler and the other investigators struggled to maintain their 'space alien' speculations. Even though they used Olympic-standard conclusion-jumping to keep their ufological tunnel reality intact, they were still forced to admit that:

> At certain points, Betty Andreasson's narrative seems to deal with a reality so alien that it can be described only in metaphors, and perhaps only understood in terms of an altered state of consciousness.[10]

This is as good a way as any of avoiding admitting the obvious: that at the hands of these entities Betty underwent what appears to have been a recognizable form of mystery school initiation. She was made to put aside her 'garments of shame', and don 'white raiment' as a prelude to being made to enter a womb-like device in order to be 'born anew'. That she was then taken to see the Emerald City of Oz only goes to reinforce further the suspicion that these entities are over-familiar with terrestrial matters to be entirely alien. Betty's abduction has undeniable affinities with astral travel because she admitted to the investigators that, at the onset of her experience, she seemed to be 'floating'. This is echoed in many abductions, in particular, that of someone crossing Ilkley Moor in Yorkshire, England, in 1987. Here, not only was a demon-like entity photographed, but a cherubic being was apparently keeping an eye on it.

This apparent ufological interface with mythology and theology is a disturbing one, because it touches directly upon the cosmological consensus of humanity, and in particular on that of the Christian West. In their Judaeo-Christian allusions, the religious ramifications of the Andreasson abduction was staggering. According to Betty's testimony, the cosmological content of her experience comprised of pre-Vatican II Roman Catholic symbology, with images of a phoenix rising from the ashes of its own, self-generated, funeral pyre as a mythological metaphor for the death and resurrection of Jesus. These are images that could not have been derived from her own subconscious because, as a 'fundamental' Christian, she had no knowledge of the metaphysical metaphor that her abductors used. This is a fact attested to by her admission that she did not even know she had been shown a phoenix until her sister explained this to her some time after her experience. From this it can only be concluded that the UFO occupants wanted to be taken for God. This is a strange ambition for EBEs, but totally understandable in context of the survival of our Cretaceous creator, the intelligent dinosaur.

It is impossible to move away from the Andreasson abduction without pointing out that her testimony entirely supported the thesis that UFOs and those who drive around in them are from the hidden kingdom inside the Earth. Meantime, her baffled investigators were single-mindedly seeking ET by asking leading questions designed to elicit ETH-friendly answers. Betty Andreasson calmly offered information that strongly supported the possibility of a hollow Earth by saying, 'I could have been inside the Earth.'[11] Unwilling to accept this answer, her interrogators continued to press for answers interpretable in ET terms. Sceptics assure us that the hypnotized will invariably produce answers in accordance with what the hypnotist wants to hear. Betty Andreasson, while conforming to this by agreeing that she left this Earth, apparently suddenly changed tack and told the investigators, 'I believe we were in the centre of the Earth.'[12] Although, with this answer, the writing was on the wall for the ETH, the investigators, with heads crammed full of unwarranted ET assumptions, persisted in speculating about the place they thought (hoped more like) Betty had been taken to. They surmised it could have been like a large garage. A multi-storey car-park in the sky? Or did the investigators secretly hope, in their science-fiction souls, that a construction similar to the Death Star was orbiting the Earth? I suggest they were clutching at exo-straws, and had they but known that Betty was going to give them the bird (phoenix), so to speak, they would not have continued with their hypnotic investigations. From their ET point of view the Death Star would have been infinitely preferable to what they did get: an entity invitation to assume the percipient had been talking to God. Betty certainly believed she had, but the investigators were too immersed in trying to prove the ETH correct to be bothered about conversations with God, so the religious symbolism that actually dominated the abduction was written off by them as being 'non-related' to the overall experience. However, Raymond Fowler, the chief investigator, was forced to lay aside his ET preconceptions long enough to wonder if 'it was a deliberate deception on the part of the aliens to make human beings believe in a UFO–Religion connection'.[13] I go along with the idea that the entities were trying, via Betty, to inculcate a belief in a UFO–religion connection, but I don't quite see why that must necessarily be considered a deception.

The UFO–religion connection has a fairly long pedigree. Many readers, I am sure, will be aware of the strong ufological link with the 'Gods' of ancient India. These beings, if the Sanskrit accounts are to be believed, regularly engaged in air combat with *vimanas* which, judging by the descriptions in the ancient texts, were some kind of saucer-like attack aircraft. It has to be suspected that these ancient Indian legends hark back to the days before the Cretaceous period cut off and in their present form are only a garbled account of races and realities long since perished from the face of the planet. But, of course, the clearest UFO–religion connection comes when we consider the content of the Bible, both Old and New Testaments. That these texts are really nothing more than pre-scientific contactee narratives is abundantly clear once we disabuse our minds of the nonsense that a universal deity needs the sychophantic adulation of an infinitely inferior life form to keep him/her/it happy. At this remove in time, it is impossible to prove satisfactorily that the 'pillars of fire', 'smoking fire pot', 'burning bush' and a host of similar pre-scientific descriptive references in the Old Testament specifically refer to appearances of UFO technology. There is, however, at least one reference of this sort that has been analysed: 'The results obtained show us a space vehicle which beyond any doubt is not only technically feasible but in fact is very well designed to fulfil its functions and purpose.'[14] Apparently astonished by his own findings, the analyser remarks, 'What remains fantastic is that such a spacecraft was a tangible reality more than 2500 years ago!'[15] The subject of this analysis was the strange object described by the Prophet Ezekiel. While its competent conclusions leave no doubt that Ezekiel's 'vision' represented a technology far in advance of anything available to the humans of those times, I still feel that it was something of a leap of faith to call this ancient UFO a spaceship, because it was only ever seen and described by Ezekiel while operating 'in atmosphere'. Even so it was the one white crow that practically proves that something more than human was operating on Earth in times past. A further point of note is that Ezekiel prefaced a significant number of his 'contactee' accounts with a phraseology that seems to inject – as with any number of modern UFO abductees – an incongruous element of OOBE into an otherwise objective account. It is this astral travel element, which the analyst Joseph

Blumrich adroitly avoids addressing, that unerringly identifies Ezekiel's experience as a confrontation with what, in our century, has come to be known as 'UFO occupants'. Therefore, in the light of what has already been argued about the 'inner earth' origins of those UFO-phenomenon related individuals, Ezekiel's observation of the UFO approaching 'out of the North' perhaps assumes a greater significance than Blumrich gave it, when he speculates that the spaceship of Ezekiel came from a 'mothership' in Polar orbit. As the Ezekiel account cannot be taken in isolation from the other Biblical material indicating alien (in the non-human rather than ET sense) activity on earth, caution must be exercised before attributing it all to the mystical machinations of deity.

Turning now to the New Testament, it becomes easier to indicate the UFO-phenomenon relatedness of an allegedly historic happening. From what I know of UFO-phenomenon initiated interactions, I can accept the literal accuracy of the New Testament account. As we all know, it started with the possible abduction and definite impregnation of Mary. As 'God' is a spirit and therefore impotent, it is just about possible to suppose that Baby Jesus was some kind of clone. However, in view of what Bud Hopkins's investigations have unearthed in present-day America, it becomes more reasonable to assume that the donor was an intelligent dinosaur lookalike. This would also explain Jesus's psychic powers, because it is probable that seemingly paranormal powers come naturally to the 'greys', whom I suspect of being somehow genetically related to ourselves. These recognizably UFO-related correlations could be expanded throughout the New Testament narrative. The meandering nocturnal 'star' of Bethlehem, the 'transfiguration' of Jesus and, in particular, the 'darkening' of the Sun (a UFO-related phenomemon that we shall meet again in the next chapter). Also there are the strong ufological correlations to consider in what happened after Jesus's alleged 'resurrection' and his consequent ascension into 'heaven' in a cloud.

As we know 'clouds' of a particular kind are attributed to the presence of God in the Old Testament, so it should come as no surprise that in respect of this New Testament 'cloud' even a committed Christian apologist has found it necessary to speculate that 'this cloud was no ordinary cloud'.[16] If that was the case, what was it, then? According to this same Christian commentator:

> The Ascension cloud was the same UFO which led the Israelites through the Red Sea, gave Moses the Commandments, carried Elijah to heaven, 'descended' like a dove at the baptism of Jesus, perhaps carrying him bodily into the wilderness, as he was carried bodily away at the Ascension.[17]

All of which tends inevitably to indicate that either whatever operates as the UFO phenomenon is in fact 'God', or something is trying to take unfair advantage of our racial tendency to cosmological gullibility to bring about a situation where, at no real risk to itself, it will completely control the human race on earth.

Taking this point of view, it can be argued that, in terms of assisting in its thrust to world domination, the UFO phenomenon considered Jesus a complete failure. It seems unarguable that he expected the hosts from heaven to rescue him from crucifixion, and when they did not turn up he was disappointed – to put it mildly. Even so, there is little doubt that the historical Jesus did in fact survive the crucifixion. Robert Graves and Joshua Podro, in the sequel to *The Nazarene Gospel Restored* titled *Jesus in Rome*, advanced evidence that indicated that Jesus was seen in Rome only shortly after his crucifixion. From there he apparently went to Kashmir, in India, taking his mother with him. Here, they both died and were buried, according to A. Faber-Kaiser in *Jesus Died in Kashmir*. This view is reinforced by the overwhelming evidence presented in *Jesus Lived in India* by Holger Kersten. If the historical Jesus is buried in Kashmir, who was ascended into heaven? Reading the account of Jesus's resurrection in the New Testament, one cannot help noticing the strange fact that he was initially unrecognizable to even his closest follower, Mary Magdalen, who apparently mistook him for a 'gardener'. This strange unrecognizability is reinforced by his meeting of his erstwhile followers, who did not recognize him until they broke bread together. Could this be because the individual who stayed around in Jerusalem was an impostor of some kind? A UFO occupant whose hypnogogic powers took a while to impress themselves on the Apostles? Could what happened after the resurrection represent an entity attempt to keep the belief system initiative going until a replacement for the historical Jesus could be found? A real ego-driven individual, a rabble-rouser . . . like Saul of Tarsus?

Until the 'conversion' of St Paul, Christianity was going nowhere. All it had amounted to was just another beyond the fringe sect of Judaism. The only impact it had was on the congregations and the priests of the synagogues where its adherents preached within their precincts. Paul of Tarsus had got himself a job as a kind of bounty hunter/witchfinder general and was persecuting the Christians. Self-serving, opinionated, arrogant and ambitious, he was a prime target for the intelligence that operates as the UFO phenomenon. On the road to Damascus it finally caught up with him:

> It seems most consistent with the other Biblical material to assume that the same type of 'bright cloud' space vehicle [why, necessarily a space vehicle?] which had led the Israelites through the Red Sea [and had spoken to Moses out of the middle of a glowing thicket to call him] and which spoke to Elijah outside of the cave [Elijah covered his face because of the brightness; the bushes shielded the eyes of Moses], the UFO which was the source of the voice at the Transfiguration which said, 'This is my beloved Son,' and which undoubtedly was the vehicle in which Christ was taken away at the Ascension, was also the UFO which hovered over Paul and his companions on the Damascus Road.[18]

The result was that Paul's fanaticism was put to the service of spreading the belief system favoured by the UFO phenomenon. He eventually replaced the original 'christianity' with Paulianity and the Christianity that was connected with the historical Jesus of Nazareth perished permanently with the destruction of Jerusalem. This, if we judge by the intervention of the UFO phenomenon, was what had been intended from the first. However, as this book is not intended as a treatise on comparative religion, you must follow that up for yourselves if you want to. The point being made here is that it appears that 'religion' of a sort was, and indeed *is*, the name of the UFO game. The intelligence behind UFO manifestations appears to be a 'belief generator', a 'tunnel-reality reinforcer' *par excellence*, and it is in this aspect of its operations that it most clearly indicates its Earthly origins. No genuine extraterrestrial entities could so consistently, and convincingly, personify the eschatological expectations of the cosmologically challenged masses. The way it is happening one could be forgiven for suspecting that we are witnessing the acting out of a predetermined Cecil B. De Mille-style trilogy: *God* (the Old Testament), *Son of God* (the New Testament) and, still to come, the ultimate blockbuster, *Return of the Son of God*. To begin to suspect seriously that a UFO-related apocalyptic operation is under way, one has only to note that:

> Eschatological literature makes Israel the focal point of attention. Without the appearance of Israel with the return of the Jews to their homeland, Biblical prophecy could not take place. It is therefore rather interesting to contemplate the virtual explosion of UFOs in the modern era (June 24, 1947) coincidental with the founding of the Jewish state. In fact, if we consider the 1947 United Nations resolution establishing a Jewish and Palestinian area, the UFO and the founding of Israel were synchronous.[19]

This is not the same as saying that the Israeli people's god is the Universal Creator, nor that the historical Jesus was his son. It just might indicate that 'something', by manipulating the masses via ego-inflationary tunnel realities fostered by the deliberate perversion and misinterpretation of the basic tenets of the Judaeo-Christian religion, is attempting to get humanity to co-operate in its own destruction. To make this point, that of UFO hostility even when the phenomenon is striving to convey the appearance of being benevolent, it becomes necessary to find an instance of UFO entities deliberately masquerading in religious guise and using their UFO technology to reinforce that deception, while at the same time engaging in activities designed to be terminal for their percipients.

References

[1] *Dimensions*, Jacques Vallée (Souvenir Press, 1988).
[2] *UFOs: Key to Earth's Destiny*, compiled by Winfield S. Brownell (Legion of Light Publications, 1980).
[3] ibid.
[4] *The Archetype Experience*, Gregory L. Little (Rainbow Books, 1984).
[5] ibid.

[6] *Round Trip to Hell in a Flying Saucer*, Cecil Michael (Roofhopper Enterprises, 1971).
[7] ibid.
[8] *The Andreasson Affair*, Raymond F. Fowler (Bantam, 1980).
[9] ibid.
[10] ibid.
[11] ibid.
[12] ibid.
[13] ibid.
[14] *The Spaceships of Ezekiel*, Josef F. Blumrich (Corgi, 1974).
[15] ibid.
[16] *The Bible and Flying Saucers*, Barry H. Downing (Sphere, 1973).
[17] ibid.
[18] ibid.
[19] Little, op. cit.

CHAPTER 9
BVM or BEM?

IT WILL no doubt come as a shock to some to learn that an archetypal religious visionary figure like the Blessed Virgin Mary (BVM) has ufological associations going far beyond the merely coincidental. The French ufologist Gilbert Cornu demonstrated the close correlation between visions of the Virgin and sightings of UFOs when he proved that there was 'a marked upsurge in visions of the Virgin in 1947'.[1] The UFO/BVM correlation indicated by Cornu's work was independently confirmed by a similar study by an Italian UFO group which used a different statistical sampling to make the same point. The conclusion arrived at by both studies – that of a connection between visions of the Virgin and UFO manifestations – led one noted ufologist to speculate that

> The things we see as UFOs are really something associated with the Virgin Mary *or*
> The Entity we see as the Virgin Mary is really something to do with UFOs *or*
> There is some common factor that makes some people see, or think they see, the Virgin Mary, while others see, or think they see, UFOs.[2]

But there is another possibility: that this UFO/BVM correlation is only to be expected once it is accepted that, on the basis of Biblical descriptions, the UFO phenomenon has apparently had this same cosmological connection since the days of Moses . . . at least. In many ways, the Old and New Testaments can be read as the ongoing documentation of a series of interconnected contactee experiences. So it should come as no surprise – at least to ufologists – that Biblical-style initiatives would still be operative in this scientifically secular age; that the voice that now speaks from the 'burning bush' is allegedly that of the BVM, rather than that of Jehovah is apropos of nothing, because we have only ever had their word that they are who they claim to be. Moreover, that the UFO phenomenon, an allegedly extraterrestrial manifestation, is demonstrably the common denominator connecting the appearances of these two allegedly 'spiritual' personages is indicative of origins other than supernatural on the one hand, and of extraterrestrial on the other. This leaves only one viable option open, and while it might be impossible now to prove convincingly a UFO–religious vision correlation in Biblical times, the same cannot be said to apply to the more modern manifestations of the BVM.

The event that confirms the connection between visions of the Virgin and the UFO phenomenon – with all the cosmological ramifications such a correlation implies – is the 'Dancing Sun' of Fatima, in Portugal. When this event occurred in 1917, such 'scientific' explanations as 'crowd hysteria', 'mass hallucination, 'Jesuitical farce' and 'a plot to overthrow the Government', were invoked to debunk the reports of the 'Solar Prodigy' which circulated in the Portuguese Press. Unfortunately, from extant evidence, it is quite clear that in the sky over Fatima, at solar noon on the 13 October 1917, the sun apparently boogied on down for the entertainment of a crowd of witnesses, estimated to number at least 70,000. The testimony of Dr J. Garrett, a professor from the university in nearby Coimbra, is representative of all the others recruited from witnesses at the site. According to him, 'The Sun, whirling, seemed to loosen itself from the firmament and advance threateningly upon the Earth as if to crush us with its huge fiery weight.'[3] Reports of this event by reporters confirmed the reality of what had occurred. *O Seculo* trumpeted 'Terrifying Event! How the Sun Danced at Midday in the Sky at Fatima!', while *O Dia* reported, 'The clouds were rent and the Sun like a silver disc began to revolve on itself and zigzag in a circle.' This description was echoed in other news-papers, in particular *Ordem*, which said that the sun seemed to be 'moving very fast and spinning: at times it seemed to be loosed from the sky and to approach the Earth'. As all these reports were derived from witnesses at the site, they might still leave room for accusations of Press exaggeration of hysterical imaginings fired by a mixture of pious gullibility and mass hallucination. These accusations can be refuted by pointing out that this same event was witnessed by others who were up to 30 miles (48 km) away from Fatima:

> At least one eyewitness, the poet Alphonso Lopes Viera, saw the miracle from a distance of 30 miles – at the ocean town of San Pedro der Muel. The author [Francis Johnson] has discovered first hand that the miracle was seen in Pombal, some 32 miles to the north. Investigations have proved that it was visible over an area of approximately 32 miles by 20.[4]

Therefore, it can be safely accepted that the so-called 'Solar Prodigy' did in fact occur, so some real attempt should be made to find out what caused the sun to roll around heaven that day. That it wasn't our parent star is obvious. Had the meandering monstrosity over Fatima really been the sun, then not only would the Earth have been adversely affected, but the entire solar system would have been devastated by the orbital and gravitational imbalances initiated by the aberrant behaviour of its central body. That the sun eventually returned to its 'accustomed place' after the display would have in no way mitigated the severity of the cataclysms caused by its previous movements. Therefore, as we are all still here, it can be assumed that the object that danced in the sky over Fatima was not the sun. More to the point, astronomical observatories recorded nothing untoward in the sun's behaviour on that day. Stupendous as the sight must have been to those who witnessed it, it still must have been only a localized event. So, pious gullibility and the Jesuits notwithstanding, what in heaven's name was it that convinced thousands that the sun was crashing down upon their heads?

It would be very easy for me to answer – quick as a flash – a UFO! But, as the acronym UFO stands for Unidentified Flying Object, to attempt to identify the Fatima object in this way is tantamount to an admission that I have no idea what it was, which is not strictly true. To identify the Fatima object properly, all that is necessary is to address the witness testimony in a secular rather than sacred state of mind. In all the eye-witness testimony collected, the object is defined as looking like 'a matt silver disc', with 'a clearly defined edge', which was seen to be 'rotating'. The most interesting remark came from a Miss N., who was 'an ordinary member of the Church of England who was not just sceptical but "disliked" everything to do with Roman Catholicism'.[5] Apparently she was not at the site by choice, but she had been compelled to accompany her Portuguese employer. It can, therefore, be surmised with certainty that she would be immune to any communicable papish 'pious gullibility' affecting others at the site. Yet, in her testimony she quite clearly confirmed what others witnessed when she told Captain C.C. Osborne that:

> The rain suddenly stopped – stopped, as if cut off by a tap. The heavy clouds did not 'roll away', but through a hole in them you saw the sun. It was the colour of stainless steel.[6]

She apparently emphasized her description at this juncture by pointing to a kitchen knife made of stainless steel and stating that the 'sun' appeared to be made of that same material. She went on to confirm that she watched this peculiar 'sun' – 'spin round, and stop, and spin round again'.[7] To hindsight, and late twentieth-century imaginations expanded by nearly half a century of ufological documentation, it is obvious that Miss N. and the others were not describing the sun, but were calling upon the only mental image available to them even to attempt a description of what they had actually seen. All one has to do is replace the word 'sun' with the word 'object' to indicate unequivocally what was deliberately masquerading as the sun in order that 'all might believe' in the BVM of Fatima. But why should a flying saucer clandestinely conspire in a masquerade, the sole purpose of which seems to have been to reinforce the parochial superstitions of a particular sectarian segment of the Roman Catholic Church? Or, looked at the opposite way, why would the alleged mother of Christ need a flying saucer to *pretend* it was the sun when – if Roman Catholic Mariolatry is correct – she had the deity that stopped the sun dead in its tracks (Joshua 10:12–14) in Old Testament times to call upon for corroboration of her claims? If, in pursuing these lines of enquiry we should discover that:

> The entities at Fatima had no real connection with the religion that later laid claim to them.[8]

then we will be left with no option but to reach the conclusion that:

> The frame of reference adopted by them must have been a sham, designed to hide or facilitate what was really going on.[9]

In this context, isn't it obvious that all the 'dancing' sun of Fatima actually proved was that you can deceive the devout into thinking the sun can manouevre itself in space without disturbing anything other than their emotional equilibrium?

Perhaps, in asserting that the Fatima object was a flying saucer of staggering size, I am getting a little carried away, because there might still be those who remain unconvinced that Fatima was a recognizably run-of-the-mill flying saucer scenario rather than a remarkable religious vision. For the doubters' benefit, I will now draw attention to the flying saucer peripherals that surrounded and accompanied the appearances of the 'lady of light' at Fatima. One peripheral effect, in particular, is conclusive of the peripheral effect, in particular, is conclusive of the Fatima episode being a flying saucer interaction. If it had just been the main percipients, the three children Jacinta, Francisco and Lucia, who 'saw things', then the apparitions at Fatima could have been dismissed as a product of puerile piousness. But throughout the entire period, some six months in all, persons attending the site reported phenomena (i.e., 'sourceless buzzing noises', 'globes of light', 'self-impelled clouds' and 'flashes of light' – all of which have been reported in a UFO context) clearly indicating that flying saucery rather than Roman Catholicism was responsible for the ongoing interaction. But as circumstantially convincing as these other 'side' effects would seem to be, there is one in particular that, in conjunction with the testimony regarding the 'stainless steel dancing sun', unerringly identifies the Fatima episode as an undeniable flying saucer, 'contactee-'type confrontation.

During the penultimate encounter of the 13 September 1913, after a moving 'luminous globe' had been seen by the crowds at the site, there descended from above a very peculiar precipitation. Later sanctimonious speculations transformed this strange down-fall into 'rose petals'; which only goes to prove that you can deceive all the people all of the time – if you get them to conspire with you in their own deception. According to the testimony of those who were there that day, most of what fell seemingly from

within 'a great jet of light' high up in the sky, never actually
reached the ground – most of it dissipating as it descended. What
did reach the ground evaporated at a touch. Identical downfalls,
which evaporated in the atmosphere and volatolized on contact,
have been seen descending in the wake of clearly visible flying
saucers – principally in France, at Graulhet, Oloron and Gaillac.
Perhaps the best, and most typical of all the reports containing
examples of rose petal-type precipitations, are those which
occurred in Oloron and Gaillac in 1952. These two occurrences
were ten days apart, but absolutely identical. On 17 October
1952, at about 13.00, a strange cavalcade crossed the sky above
Oloron. It consisted of a cylindrical object, tilted at a 45-degree
angle in the direction of flight, and several smaller objects which
zigzagged swiftly around the main object. As they crossed the
clear blue sky, 'All these strange objects left very long trails which
disintegrated and drifted slowly groundwards'.[10] Witnesses to
this incident were many and varied, including the mayor of the
village of Géronce and a shooting party in the valley of Josbaig.
As Aimé Michel pointed out in respect of explanations for
the affair,

> Must we resort to 'collective hallucination'? But if so, it would
> be nothing less than miraculous that a large number of people
> over a wide area should think they see precisely the same
> spectacle, a crazy if unmistakable spectacle at the very same
> time![11]

His comments apply equally to the 'rose petals' and the 'Dancing
Sun' of Fatima. Then it happened all over again. At approximately
17.00 on 27 October an identical aerial parade passed over the
town of Gaillac. The same cylinder at the same 45-degree angle,
the same smaller objects darting around it and, finally, the
peculiar precipitation that came to be known (with a degree of
synchronicity that would surely have sent Jung into raptures) as
'Threads of the Virgin'. This time there were at least a hundred
witnesses, including two non-commissioned officers of the
gendarmerie. As identical effects imply identical causes, it becomes
inevitable that at Fatima on the 13 September the flying saucer
phenomenon was present in the sky above the Cova de Iria,
which begs the question: what was the alleged mother of Jesus
doing in the company of alleged aliens? It is quite obvious from the

evidence that at Fatima we have a case where the flying saucer phenomenon has been caught red-handed promoting itself as a bona fide 'religous vision', and deliberately using recognizable flying saucer technology to lend substance to that deception. But to what possible purpose? Well, can it be only coincidence that very shortly after the 'apparitions' had ended, two of the main percipients, young Francisco and Jacinta, died miserable and agonizing deaths (and this after the BVM had promised they would not be harmed) from a mystery disease that eventually decimated the human race? Records showed that not even the Black Death of the Middle Ages had been as lethal, because during October 1918, 'The total deaths throughout the world were estimated between 15–25 million – the greatest visitation ever experienced by the human race.'[12] For those who might like to put it all down to 'coincidence', it must be pointed out that the BVM told the two victims that she would 'come soon' to take the to 'heaven'. She must have known how she would 'take them', especially as she also, on this same occasion, told the third visionary, Lucia, that she would live on, which is what happened: Lucia – now a nun – is still alive. From this it can be deduced that at Fatima the phenomenon infected the two youngest children, then by drawing crowds into contact with them, exposed the entire human race to the virus that 'spread throughout the world infecting entire populations, with a death toll in excess of twenty one million persons'.[13] So, you can now understand why it has to be considered imperative to unravel the mystery of the UFO-religious connection, especially as exemplified by the various appearances of the Queen of Flying Saucery – the BVM.

For some reason, the UFO phenomenon, disguised as the BVM, seems to be always on the look-out for fresh percipients. From a number of sources I have learned that there are over 50 'appearances' in progress worldwide. This is a state of affairs that is probably 'situation normal' if we presume that BVM works according to the demands of statistical probability, which dictates that only a certain percentage of her ploys will meet with the kind of success she had at Fatima. In this context, I was to come across one of her less publicized 'appearances' during which she herself was to confirm her connection with flying saucers. It was while investigating another 'entity' report that I found out that the BVM had put in an appearance in West Yorkshire, England. The main witness, a woman approaching pensionable age came to me with a story that seemed to have strong affinities with other visions of the BVM. After extracting from me the usual undertakings to preserve her anonymity, this witness, whom I shall call 'Marion', described how at 20.00 one evening in September 1978 she had seen a 'figure' she took to be the BVM as if projected in some way by the dying rays of the setting sun on to her next door neighbour's wall. To say that she was astonished is probably to understate her reaction. She was not, she said, the first to see this 'apparition'. Her friend had seen it on an earlier occasion, but Marion had not believed her when she had been told. Then came Marion's own sighting of:

> a petite young woman, dressed in a brilliant white gown that covered her from throat to toes, and which was held at the waist by a silken knotted rope similar in design to those which used to be worn by Roman Catholic nuns as part of their more sombre 'habits'. Her head was covered by a pale blue veil that came down to her shoulders but did not obscure her hair, which was 'glowing brunette' and of a fairly modern style. Apparently being cut to 'turn under' at ear level. On the apparition's head was a 'crown' or 'diadem' or 'tiara' of unusual brilliance.[14]

It was this crown that captured most of Marion's initial attention, because it seemed to be composed of several 'jewels of unearthly magnificence'. Even when describing them as light blue, dark blue, amber, green, red, mauve and turquoise, Marion insisted that they were several orders of magnitude more 'vibrant' than their Earthly equivalents. This resplendent figure stood close to a laburnum tree in her neighbour's garden, and appeared to be surrounded by 'a glowing golden aura', seemingly made up of the sun's rays. Although this apparition, like the one at Knock in Ireland, appeared to be 'projected' (albeit three-dimensionally) against her neighbour's wall, it was not static but smiled and gestured to Marion as if aware of her scrutiny. Marion claimed to have seen this 'apparition' on several subsequent occasions – once in the company of a priest who admitted to her that he too could see it – and that smiles and 'gestures' were forthcoming on each occasion. One of these 'gestures', which apparently involved the vision holding up eight fingers, was particularly disturbing to

her. I later learned why, but I would not have done had not the
witness asked me:

> 'D'you think that flying saucers have anything to do with the
> end of the world and the Judgement?'
> 'What makes you ask that?' I countered.
> 'Well,' replied my witness, *'she* has told me they're
> coming.'[15]

A mass landing prophesied by the BVM? I thought such things
were left to UFO contactees/abductees. The cultural consequences
that would ensue in even considering the possibility that flying
saucers may be intimately connected with the creation and
maintenance of, arguably, *the* major religious mythology of this
planet, are almost too terrible to contemplate. Yet, the possibility
is there, and – if real – cannot remain ignored for ever. Consider
the following. The BVM appears to Marion, who claims real-time
visionary interaction with her, which leads to an OOBE
experience initiated by the BVM appearing in her bedroom.
During this 'visit', Marion was allegedly taken from her bed to
the bedroom window, through which she watched flying saucers
skywriting the date for the end of the world. This indicates to me
that there is possibly something more sinister than interstellar
invasion being covered up in ufology. My suspicion is that the
real secret of saucery is to be found somewhere in the Vatican
archives, where it was locked away after being read in 1960. How
else can you explain the amazing volte-face in the Roman Catholic
Church's attitude after the final secret of Fatima had been opened
and read (but never to this day made public) by the Pope? In the
years leading up to 1960 the increasingly insular Catholic Church
got much mariological mileage out of the so-called 'third secret' of
Fatima until, according to the newspaper *A Voz*: 'The entire
world, Catholic and non-Catholic, looks with anxiety towards the
fateful year of 1960.'[16] From personal experience, I can confirm
that the clergy lost no opportunity to drive the fear of God into
their congregations. Almost openly, they claimed that when the
'secret' was opened and made public by the Pope, the entire
world would be forced to bend the knee to Rome. That great
expectations were abroad in Catholicism is evinced by the fact
that the convening Second Vatican Council had been announced

by Pope John XXIII in 1959 – *before* the anticipated opening of the 'secret'. Unfortunately, subsequent events prove that great expectations led to even greater disappointments. Instead of the expected ratification of Roman Catholicism, there emanated from the Vatican a silence that spoke volumes about what had not been in the envelope when it had been opened. But what had it contained? Well, when I tell you that the kind of information that a vested interest will not reveal about itself is the sort that would be destructive of its power base, you can probably guess for yourselves. All I will say is that whatever was in the 'third secret of Fatima', it probably possessed, at the very least, the potential to render not just the Catholic faith redundant. So, the Vatican had no option but to suppress the 'secret' and endure the embarrassment provoked by its silence on the very subject it had – only days before – been extremely voluble. Speculations by orthodox theologians, or even ufologians, about the actual content of the 'third secret of Fatima' are unlikely to bear much factual fruit, because they are mostly based in the very apocalyptic delusions fostered by the 'vision'. Therefore, they are likely to be arguing from false parameters from the start. The trick is not to accept the manifestation in its own terms. Just look at the ones through whom the BVM has chosen transmit the allegedly important 'message to humankind' of oncoming doom and disaster. Equally indicative that something other than genuine 'warnings' are involved is the fact that the whole process is ongoing. The BVM (or incredibly advanced alien) turns up regularly to 'admonish' the 'faithful' that there will be 'trouble' if the 'message' is ignored *this time*. A correspondent has recently made me aware that the BVM is now stirring things up at Conyers, in the USA, and is attempting to rekindle the flames of an old xenophobia by alleging that 'Russia, China and North Korea would form "a deadly trio"'.[17] Her appearances, once again on the thirteenth of each month, are apparently accompanied by recognizable 'ufological' special effects – in particular, the 'storm' that allegedly accompanied the appearance on the 13 May 1993, at which time the BVM is credited with the following unspecific generalization, and completely meaningless 'warning to America' that 'you are going deeper and deeper into darkness'.[18] Surely if you wanted to 'warn America' of some real danger, you would go straight to the top and would give gullible nonentities a wide berth in case any connection with them damaged your prospects of being taken seriously by those with real influence? So what is the BVM doing at Conyers? Certainly not 'warning America' I venture to suggest, presuming, of course, that the whole affair isn't some kind of holy hoax for monetary gain. As with the various ufological 'tunnel realities', the proponents of the 'tunnel reality' of visions of the Virgin leap to their conclusions from the apex of an edifice composed of their own unwarranted assumptions, abetted and encouraged by a phenomenon that can, and does, present itself in any guise necessary for the forwarding of its main objective. The question those egotistic nonentities, who see nothing farcical in being 'chosen' to transmit a message of supreme importance to the entire human race, should ask themselves is: Why me? The answer can only be that they are a 'mark' distinguished by their innate gullibility in believing that anything truly superior would 'choose' them to transmit a message of such profound importance. They are more to be pitied than encouraged.

If, as is strongly suspected, these 'appearances' are not motivated by some kind of alien or heavenly altruism, what can they be motivated by? If the creatures engaging in these activities are as alien as many suggest they are, then it has to be considered as possible that their motives might not be amenable to human interpretation. But what if they are not as alien as some suppose? Is it possible that paranormal phenomena as a whole (i.e., UFOs, angels, aliens, BVMs, etc.) represent an ongoing attempt by some non-human life form to gain, or perhaps regain, control of the human race? The idea that the UFO phenomenon, and therefore by implication the whole panapoly of the paranormal, is some kind of 'control system' has been mooted by Jacques Vallée, who suggests, 'It is human belief that is being controlled and conditioned.'[19] I mean, how close can you come and still be wide of the mark? Perhaps as close as Brad Steiger, who apparently leans to the opinion that:

> The U.F.O. Phenomenon can be fitted to the hypothesis that they represent the pre-natal care of the Earthman by a linked superbeing, in preparation for the forthcoming linkage of the human species and the birth of another linked superbeing.[20]

I cannot accept this. From the extant evidence – especially that pertaining to the BVM – it is an obviously unwarranted assumption that 'someone up there loves us'. It seems more likely that, in accordance with the observed natural order of things, the UFO phenomenon is pursuing its own agenda, which sometimes makes it behave deliberately in a way that we interpret as altruistic. That this misinterpretation of motive is intended by the manifestation is argued by the fact that percipients are always spoon fed whatever ego-supportive superstitions are favoured by whatever parochial tunnel reality they subscribe to. Christians see 'angels' or the BVM, spiritualists see 'the dear departed', theosophists see 'ascended adepts', and the less spiritually committed see flying saucers. The clever part is that individuals see and hear phenomena in accordance with the expectations of their 'secret' beliefs, rather than those which, for society's sake, they publicly subscribe to. In actual fact, from the evidence it is possible to deduce that the human race is indeed being controlled by a manipulation of its beliefs. But as it is equally arguable that the phenomenon created these beliefs in the first place, where does that leave us?

The clue, perhaps, is to be found in the statements attributed to the BVM which would indicate she was making a claim to deity. At Fatima, she continually stressed that humanity must make reparation for sins against her 'immaculate heart'. The definition of sin is 'a transgression against God's known will', so make of that what you will. But bear in mind that at La Salette in France, in 1846, her claim was quite unequivocal because, according to the witnesses, she said, 'I gave you six days for work, I kept the seventh for myself.'[21] A strange statement for one who has also encouraged (by her incessant references to 'my son') a 'belief' in her as the mother of Jesus Christ . . . the Mary of the Gospel. Perhaps we should accept that the BVM is just another personification by a phenomenon that has attempted to claim the worship of humankind by appearing as a 'burning bush', 'a pillar of fire', etc. in Old Testament times, the BVM and assorted 'saints' in New Testament times, and which, in accordance with the public superstitions engendered by the new religion of science is, even now, attempting to control individuals via their 'beliefs' in the existence of 'advanced aliens'. Then, such an agenda is to be expected; even that in the USA, where in Hangar 18 (where else?) the living aliens that were retrieved along with their crashed saucer(s) are allegedly now claiming to be the 'creators' of humankind. I find all this more than probable as it fits in with the strategy that has obviously been employed to regain our submission these past 5,000 years (or more if certain records are to be believed), and is certainly in line with the claims, put forward on their behalf by a contactee calling himself 'Rael'. In the 'Rael' revelations, we see again yet another nonentity 'chosen' to give humanity the kind of message that would be difficult to get across if 'channelled' through an accepted scientific authority. It can therefore be suspected that something other than 'getting the message through to humankind' is the object of the exercise. Apparently, the 'Elohim' (an alien race rather than a monotheistic deity) is now wanting – through Rael – to let us know that they created *all* life on earth, made us 'in their own image', invented *all* our religions, and sent *all* the prophets to update them as and when they deemed this was necessary. But now they can't land on Earth because they haven't got a bit of land to call their own. They want us to build them an embassy – just as the BVM wants us to build churches?

Once you admit the probability that the Rael revelation (and others essentially similar) is no different in substance from that given to percipients of the BVM or Moses up the mountain – in that it encourages human beings to hand over their autonomy to a self-proclaimed 'superior being' – you can immediately see that the problem of the UFO phenomenon is much older than the 40 or so years it has been publicly pondered in the media and cult fanzines. The polarity it has generated among those drawn to its study unerringly identifies it as a basically religious rather than secular mystery. The very fact that it can be 'believed' and 'disbelieved' with equal emotional intensity shows that we are dealing with superstition and not science. It is indicative of imposture that every 'revelator' is isolated from every other, and apparently subscribes to a different 'superior' being(s), who seem always unaware of each other's existence. Vallée and others are probably correct when they claim the UFO phenomenon is a 'control system', but they fall into the trap set by the phenomenon when they presume this is designed to bring some ill-defined benefit to the human race. As with her more 'scientific siblings, the BVM is apparently interested in only one thing: the reduction of the human race to the kind of superstitious serfdom that would make us more amenable to the manipulations of our 'masters', and that makes her more likely to be BEM rather than BVM.

References

[1] *Visions, Apparitions, Alien Visitors*, Hilary Evans (Book Club Associates, 1984).
[2] ibid.
[3] *Fatima: A Close Encounter of the Worst Kind*, David Barclay (Mark Saunders, 1987).
[4] *Fatima: The Great Sign*, Francis Johnston (Augustine Publishing Co., 1980).
[5] Barclay, op. cit.
[6] *The Message of Fatima*, C. C. Martindale (S. J. Burns, Oates & Washbourne, 1950).
[7] ibid.
[8] Barclay, op. cit.
[9] Barclay, op. cit.
[10] *The Truth About Flying Saucers*, Aimé Michel (Corgi, 1958).
[11] ibid.
[12] *Influenza: The Last Great Plague*, W. I. B. Beveridge (Heinemann, 1977).
[13] *Plagues and People*, W. H. McNeill (Blackwell, 1977).
[14] 'The BVM in West Yorkshire', David Barclay, *The UFO Debate*, No. 4, August 1990.
[15] ibid.
[16] Barclay (1987), op. cit.
[17] Author's personal files (1994).
[18] The Journal From Conyers, May 1994.
[19] *UFOs: The Psychic Solution*, Jacques Vallée (Panther Books, 1977).
[20] *Gods of Aquarius*, Brad Steiger (Panther Books, 1980).
[21] *Sister Mary of the Cross*, Abbé Gouin (English edition privately published, June 1981).

CHAPTER 10
Well Saved!

ONE OF the most noticeable features of all forms of fortean 'entity' appearances, and one which is particularly prevalent and least easily explained in the case of UFO entities, is the predeliction to prophesy the onset of purely human, 'tunnel reality'-related doomsday scenarios. From their various eschatological entreaties, it becomes only too evident that, either we might be dealing with cosmic juvenile delinquents, or 'something' is testing the elasticity of our collective leg. Or, perhaps, it is that the truly intelligent life forms that probably exist in the universe at large are unable to believe that we can be so stupid as to fall for the same old 'save the world' scenario every time and continually conduct exosociological experimentation to define scientifically the limits of our racial gullibility. As much as I would like to settle for such eminently reasonable solutions, I regret I think it is more likely – in the context of the entity enigma as a whole – that the beings who reflect our parochial beliefs back to us, as if they had a basis in reality, do so to exacerbate deliberately the tribal superstitions that have been detrimental to our racial well being, and which tend to allow them to exercise power over us in the guise of whatever 'god' they personify at any given time. The pseudo-religious aspect of ufology indicates that the phenomenon that generates it is far too familiar with humankind's mythic beliefs to be as alien as those who support the ETH might like to think. I am driven to contemplate seriously the claim that the life form now presenting itself as 'ufonauts' is responsible for all religious revelation. Can it be possible that the human 'religious impulse' is based on nothing more solid than the metaphysical manipulations of a non-human life form that 'bred' us for purposes far removed from the achievement of a happy hereafter?

Disturbing no doubt to some, this prospect has to be considered as possible, especially since it can be shown that present presumptions about the existence of 'God' are really only the adult equivalent of the childish belief in the existence of Father Christmas.

The absurdities inherent in 'revelatory' scenarios are always obvious to hindsight. However, while they are in progress and evolving towards the usual disappointing denouement, a 'suspension' of the critical faculty seems to affect those involved in them. This is certainly the case when the content appeals to any cosmological prejudices they might have, as in the appearances of the BVM, or for the more 'scientific', aliens apparently doing roadside repairs to their spaceship. All entity manifestations appeal to the arrogance of the ignorant, who apparently go through life convinced of their own intellectual excellence, so they are not surprised when a 'superior intelligence' (i.e., God, aliens, BVM, etc.) singles them out to help it tell the rest of humanity where it gets off. A typical example of how much nonsense any contactee is prepared to countenance as credible is demonstrated by what happened to a group of individuals, who called themselves 'The Light Affiliates', in Burnaby, British Columbia. Their apocalyptic adventure commenced when one of them – after viewing a fairly close overflight by a UFO – began 'channeling' (a kind of sci-fi mediumship) messages to the group from a 'space brother' who lived 'in a galaxy close to our own', and who rejoiced in the name of Ox-Ho: 'The Earth, they were told by the entity, teetered on the very edge of Judgement Day.'[1] The frame of reference used by the alleged entity to facilitate this fortean farce drew heavily on the then prevailing New Age fixation with the dawning of the 'Age of Aquarius' (which we now know was a total wash out). It was garnished by the unwarranted assumptions of 'flower power' philosophy. Even so, by these means Ox-Ho managed to involve the Light Affiliates in a 'save the world' scenario that was a classic of its kind:

> The communicating entity activated twenty two year old Robin McPherson as his channel, quickly changing her name to Estelle, his little star. Aileen Steil, Robin's mother, was rechristened Magdalene; Robin's friend Sally, who was selected to serve as her 'energizer', was renamed Celeste; and a

young man who had been present during some of the early transmissions was presented with the very common contactee name of Truman Merit ('a man of true merit').[2]

Immensely impressed by all this intergalactic renaming, the group dispensed completely with its gullibility threshold, and prepared to 'save the world' by issuing the egotistic announcement, 'We of the Light Affiliates have been told to give a message of importance to all men who seek the Aquarian Age.'[3] Which inevitably provokes the question: if the message was really that important, and was intended for all men, why didn't Ox-Ho approach CNN? The answer can only be that, like the BVM who *never* approaches the Pope with her 'exhortations', the 'warning' was not the real point of the interaction. The element of non-sensicality inherent in the scenario so far presented by Ox-Ho to the Light Affiliates is quite apparent, and one wonders why any of them were deceived for one instant by it. Given that disaster was imminent, anyone with an ounce of sense would have immediately realized that salvatory strategies were redundant. According to Ox-Ho, the destruction of our planet was going to begin with a series of cataclysms which, in turn, would trigger a shift in the Earth's axis, culminating in the total destruction of the Earth 'in the physical sense'. What other sense is there I wonder? Not one that would hold out much hope for creatures such as we, I venture to suggest. Even more suggestive of some kind of space-borne spoof was the fact that all these catastrophes were promised for 22 November 1969, which gave the Light Affiliates nearly a whole month in which to marshall all the resources available to a group of nondescript individuals to help Ox-Ho 'save the world'. In effect, it was all unbelievably irrational; the most disturbing aspect being that Ox-Ho, with a familiarity that belied his allegedly intergalactic origins, casually connected the onset of the physical doomsday with the apocalyptic fantasies current at that time among proto-New Age groups concerning the dawning of the 'Age of Aquarius'. The unspoken implication of this alien attribution was that such parochial cosmology had a universal validity, which is what every 'true believer' in whatever tunnel reality wants to hear about their unimaginably underinformed tribal superstitions. My contention is that because of this 'cosmo-logically reflective' element in entity interactions, it has to be suspected that something is transpiring on planet Earth which present-day conventional wisdom cannot adequately explain away by merely muttering 'Humbug'!

It seems from the documentation that every UFO event that gets past the initial 'sighting' stage and moves on to the 'contactee/ abduction' phase possesses the potential to transform itself from a technological to a thaumaturgical experience. Telepathy, OOBE, apportation and other so-called 'spiritual' effects invade and transform the original 'scientific' setting of the ongoing experience. Then, by reinforcing whatever tunnel reality is favoured by the percipient(s), any communicating life form persuades the percipient(s) to accept the idea that they are 'specially chosen' to be privy to something important (i.e., the end of the world, a mass UFO landing, appointment to the interplanetary parliament on Uranus, etc.), the significance of which lesser mortals would be incapable of comprehending. In effect, the appeal is to the egomaniac in us all. No one is immune to such ego-inflationary blandishment. For instance, Andrija Puharich, despite his scientific credentials, has been involved twice in entity-generated cosmodramas. The most widely known of his involvements was during his sponsorship of the Geller phenomenon, at which time he apparently allowed himself to be persuaded that 'the space beings did a mind probe of all human beings and chose Puharish as the *only* human ready for their revelations.'[4] The result was that he, along with his protégé Uri Geller, entered into a 'save the world' scenario that apparently required them to rove around the Middle East in order to avert an atomic Armageddon. It obviously had the desired effect, because there has been no atomic Armageddon there – yet. It is incredibly easy to ridicule entity-generated cosmic soap operas once it is certain that whatever doom has been prophesied has not materialized. However, while they are in full spate, they carry conviction – at least for those caught up in them. In the case of the Spectra/ Hoova communications – even leaving aside the 'phenomena' that allegedly accompanied them – conviction derived from the fact that they probably 'reflected' the unspoken atomic anxieties of the Israeli Geller, and the cosmological beliefs of Puharich. Puharich, since his involvement some 20 years earlier with a Hindu medium called Dr Vinod, apparently considered himself as some kind of 'special agent' for 'The Nine' (ET, balls of light) whom he maintained ruled the Universe. Apparently, down the years 'The Nine' called upon him to operate as some kind of metaphysical James Bond, so that 'when there is trouble somewhere in the world, I go there'.[5] I know we all like to delude ourselves from time to time that we are of worth, but even then we do not go so far as to believe that our presence in an area is sufficient to avert Armageddon. However, those who are susceptible to entity entreaties obviously do, because Puharich admitted in an interview in 1974, 'Wherever there is a nuclear war coming, I usually go there.'[6] Therefore, the deduction must be that 'contactees/mediums/channels' might not be 'chosen' because they are any more 'advanced' than the rest of us, but because they are more susceptible to a certain kind of flattery. This might explain why, when the Geller phenomenon waned, Andrija Puharich got himself mixed up in an even more archetypal entity-related extravaganza which was supposed to culminate in a 'mass landing' of UFOs. On this occasion, the alleged ET communicators introduced themselves as 'The Management'. As usual the purport of the 'message', which was once again received mediumistically rather than radiophonically, was that the contactees had been 'chosen' by superior aliens (God surrogate) to tell the rest of more mundane humankind that a mass landing was imminent. Gosh! According to The Management:

> The landing would be a visible, physical event that would take place all over the planet over a period of nine days. Many different type of craft would land and beings would descend from them and be among men.[7]

The information could not have been more specific, except that it failed to indicate exactly when the landings were to begin. As they have not yet started, I must reluctantly advise you to accept the likelihood that they never will. This 'mass landing' syndrome is probably integral to Puharich's preferred personal 'tunnel reality', because the idea also turned up during the Geller years when, on 27 August 1972, a 'voice', which allegedly emanated from space intelligences in the spaceship Spectra, advised, 'We want you to prepare the earth for our landing, a mass landing on earth.'[8] The 'frame of reference' connection with Puharich was further validated when the new 'chosen' group, of which Puharich was a member, also went on an allegedly alien-inspired pilgrimage 'to help avert an imminent crisis in the Middle East by influencing the Russian leaders in Moscow by *meditation*'.[9] These two elements, the 'mass landing' and the 'psychic pilgrimage', point up the possibility that every so-called 'alien' initiative – from The Nine, through Spectra and Rhombus 4D, to The Management – probably derived solely from Puharich's personal cosmology. Apart from the explicit information about the coming 'mass landing' nothing of note was transmitted by The Management. The 'communications' consisted of a cosmological concoction of elements from the various tunnel realities of the group, presented in such a way to engage their ego mechanisms by reinforcing their own opinions about themselves and the superstitions – theological and technological – they held dear. In effect, the pronouncements of The Management added nothing new to the sum of knowledge of the human race, despite the circumlocutions of 'Tom', a being who spoke of itself in the royal 'we' and who said, in reply to a question from Puharich about where it came from in this vast universe?: 'We come from beyond your knowledge of light. We come from the zone that you would call cold.'[10] Which is just the sort of answer you would expect from an 'advanced alien', is it not?

I have only discussed 'contacts' which were 'telepathic' or, if you prefer, 'mediumistic'. I did not include sightings of ostensibly alien enitities, so I suppose the accusation can be made that the scenarios described probably derived solely from the subconscious minds of those involved. This argument is particularly pertinent in respect of those 'contacts' in which Andrija Puharich's presence played a part – as at Ossining, USA, in the 1970s, when the allegedly 'superior beings' and apocalyptic themes introduced during his period with Uri Geller were reintroduced and elaborated. Even though it would be easy to dismiss the entire 'contactee' mythos by this relatively simple means, it would still leave unexplained those cases where an apparently bona fide UFO event ended up being more parapsychological than interplanetary. On the morning of 1 December 1987, a former policeman (ufonauts have a particular penchant for them, certainly in England) was crossing Ilkley Moor in West Yorkshire, England, when he was allegedly abducted by an LGM (little green man). Perhaps because of the way it was introduced into the genre, this abduction caused some contention in the English UFO community. You must understand, of course, that there is a strong element of undeclared scepticism in English ufology which tends to look askance at any evidence, especially photographic evidence, as a matter of course. Although I stand to be corrected, for my own reasons I accept both the incident, and the photograph proferred as proof by the percipient, as completely genuine. Although the policeman indicated he was taken into orbit in a nuts and bolts UFO, there is nevertheless every reason to suspect that it was an 'theological' rather than a 'technological' experience. The description of how he was accosted by the entity and taken to the UFO has strong elements of OOBE, because the witness, under hypnosis, said, 'I'm stuck and everything has gone fuzzy. I'm floating in the air.'[11] While 'on board' the 'saucer', he was apparently shown scenes depicting eco-disasters 'like on the news, can see lots of waste going into the river, and people like Ethiopians who are starving'.[12] There was allegedly another 'film', the content of which he was 'not allowed' (by whom?) to divulge. Perhaps this was a 'secret' similar to that given to the children at Fatima by that other 'religious' UFO-related entity, the BVM? Also indicative of the paranormal rather than interplanetary origins of the experience was the 'loud humming sound' that the policeman described as accompanying the 'saucer's' departure. This alone is sufficient to connect his untoward experience with the events at Fatima in 1917, and with even less salubrious spiritualistic phenomena. But the cosmo-logical clincher comes when he describes the 'saucer' into which he was abducted. Apparently, resting in the depression on Ilkley Moor, he saw:

what I can only describe as a large object like two silver saucers stuck together edge to edge. Some sort of box sticking out of the top was descending into the object, the humming sound I had previously heard became quite loud, and the 'saucer' shot straight up into the clouds.[13]

It was this 'box' that confirmed the essentially paranormal dimension of the experience. It appeared on the photograph and was the subject of much ufological argument about whether or not it was a natural feature – a 'reflective rock' of some kind.

Apparently, all the 'experts' were so busy parading their expertise that nobody noticed a blueish-tinged, cherubic face within the 'box'. Its gaze was directed towards the decidedly demonic looking entity in the foreground. Once this is recognized, it can be seen that, rather than facing the photographer, the 'entity' is probably looking back over its shoulder at the face. This feature is not unique to the Ilkley Moor entity report, because something similar was photographed in September 1973 on the shores of the Clearwater River in Idaho, USA. The photograph shows 'a bright blue object . . . shaped like a rounded arch, and over the top is a much larger, almost transparent arch which has a blueish tinge'.[14] The similarity did not end there, because apparently staring raptly at the 'blueish' object were 'two, three or more small greyish brown beings, more monkey-like than human-looking'.[15] There seems to have been no 'abduction' attempt on this occasion, but this does not in any way invalidate the comparisons made. The probability that ufology and theology are likely to be legs on the same elephant is further enhanced by the experiences of the Reverend Harrison Bailey who was abducted in 1951 while out hiking along State Highway 7 towards Joliet, Illinois. The 'case' is apparently quite complex because the full details of the 'abduction' did not come to light until Harrison underwent hypnosis in 1977. At that time, the investigative initiative seems to have been based on the belief that UFO= spaceship, therefore entities=space aliens. Even so, the testimony indicates that Bailey's experience was comparable to the 'abduction' on Ilkley Moor, in that he experienced physiological effects that were attributed to 'microwave radiation' by the investigators, but they could just as easily have been ascribed to OOBE. In any event, our real interest lies not with the details of the initial abduction in 1951, but with what allegedly occurred after those details had been dredged from the witness by regression hypnosis: 'Ever since recalling his experience Bailey has been bothered by weird nocturnal visitations similar to the one Betty Andreasson had after her abduction.'[16] As has already been discussed, the Andreasson abduction seemed to be more akin to a 'religious experience' than a spacenapping, even though, initially, UFO-related aliens appeared to be involved. Therefore, it seems not unreasonable in the circumstances to ask what kind of 'alien abduction' can later result in Bailey having a kind of religious vision when he recalled the details of his original UFO-related experience. He was allegedly visited by 'beings of light' who came 'to give him messages of love and peace to give to the world'.[17] Then why did he admit to the late D. Scott Rogo in 1979 that 'he didn't like the "beings of light" visiting him and that he wanted them to stop'.[18] The answer can only be that he had begun to suspect the truth about what was going on. Exactly the same seems to have happened, perhaps belatedly, to the contactee known as John Hodges (a pseudonym), himself a dedicated UFO investigator, after he had an entity encounter during the early 1970s, but not before he had astonished the investigator of his particular case by 'seemingly being on the brink of becoming a 1950-type "contactee"'.[19] This is a ufological type that is anathema to those subscribing to the ETH. Nevertheless, the investigator had to admit that Hodges had developed a 'disturbing' (well, it would be to any dyed-in-the-wool ETH believer) tendency to discourse on subjects as unscientific as God, creation, the destiny of humankind, etc. This was apparently because his experience had made him start to re-evaluate ufological material in terms of a religious revelation. So, while protesting that he was not a religious fanatic, Hodges admitted to the strong suspicion that the UFO phenomenon, from the Foo-fighters of World War 2 to his own abduction, was 'almost like a religious thing, to have people almost worship these craft'.[20] Or, more likely, the beings who drive round in them? That his 'abduction' and subsequent 'contact' were just another UFO-entity initiative to set up yet another 'save the world' scenario is evinced by the fact that he was given the usual 'prophecies' (failed) about the outbreak of World War 3 in the early 1980s and a 'mass landing' in 1987. Fortunately, or perhaps unfortunately from the ufonauts' perspective, 'Hodges luckily realized that the UFO entities are capable of misleading and deluding witnesses, and was able to catch himself before becoming a fully-fledged Messianic contactee.'[21] Consequently, the contact never moved into the 'metaphysical mode' favoured by the 'save the world' set, despite entity attempts to get the ball rolling with allusions to 'children of the galaxies', and Hodges having been 'given the seed of communicating with the galaxy'. Unfortunately, Hodges is more the exception than the rule, because most contactees never seem to consider wilful deception on the part of the communicating entities as an option. Sometimes, those individuals who 'investigate' the contactee claims of others seem willing to consider the possibility that deliberate deception might be an integral part of the 'alien' input to the interaction under investigation. For example, when the ostensibly ET-organized abduction of Betty Andreasson took an unexpected excursion into the realm of 'religious visions', the investigators were forced to consider the possibility that 'it was a deliberate deception on the part of the aliens to make human beings believe in a UFO/Religion connection'.[22] This is a pertinent question, the relevance of which to ufology as a whole is amply illustrated by what happened in the Sunderland family's interaction with the unknown. It began in 1976 when Gaynor Sunderland, still at school, was 'recruited' by the UFO phenomenon utilizing an overtly ETH frame of reference. One Saturday in July 1976, Gaynor was cycling along the Coed-On road near her home in Oakenholt on the Welsh border, when she came upon a 'landed saucer'. It is interesting to note that this object, like the one on Ilkley Moor, had a 'small square box' on its upper surface, although in this case the box was red rather than blue. Curious, Gaynor hid and watched the box until the 'aliens' hove into view. The first of these was a 'male' dressed in a seamless silver suit and carrying a weapon similar to a Star Trek 'phaser', which he obligingly demonstrated by using it to shoot holes in the ground while Gaynor watched. Then came the first hint of paranormality when, after she had made a noise and the 'alien' had obviously become aware of her, 'something deep down in her mind was aware that some alien presence had entered the private world of her thoughts'.[23] Gradually, over an extended period of time, other members of the Sunderland family were drawn into contact with the phenomenon and, with the arrival of a group calling itself Parasearch, the investigation became more spiritualistic than scientific. Perhaps because of this, and because the Sunderland family's underlying cosmological frame of reference appears to have been Wiccan, the affair eventually devolved into a kind of 'Dungeons and Dragons' format, which included 'psychic questing', an occult occupation upon which, I am relieved to say, I am not competent to comment. Of more real interest is the observation by the ufological investigators that:

The theme of the contacts involve the imminent future of this world, its race towards disaster and the role of the [Sunderland] children a a key, with the aid of aliens, towards salvation.[24]

So intellectually unpalatable did the ufologists find the 'unnecessary grandiosity' that was apparently implicit in the content of the communications that they felt themselves 'forced, therefore, to consider if what seems to be the obvious message may not in fact be the true one'.[25] The 'contactees' seemingly had no comparable misgivings, and easily accepted the experience on its own terms by making the unwarranted assumption that 'they are trying to tell us something; and it must be something very important'.[26] Which prompts me to ask why *must* it be something very important? Supposing it is important, then *important to whom – them or us?*

Despite entities' obvious affection for it, the apocalyptic aspect is one of the least emphasized attributes of ufology overall, being positively anathema to those who deal exclusively in the ETH. Yet even the 'nuts and bolts' brigade are not always immune to the seductions of the cosmology of catastrophe, as the alleged interplanetary initiative that resulted in the skycrash on Silpho Moor, near Scarborough, England, just goes to show. On the evening of 21 November 1951, a 'glowing saucer' was seen to fall on Silpho Moor, and it was eventually recovered for study by placing an advertisement in the local paper. Leaving aside the fact that the 'saucer' was only 18 in (46 cm) in diameter, weighed only 35 pounds (16 kg), and contained instead of advanced alien technology a copper tube holding a 'scroll' with a 'message' in chicken tracks, I draw attention to the claim that it had been deliberately dropped from a 'Mercurian scoutship' which had been on its way to Yeovil. The 'message', once 'decoded', turned out to be the usual warning: on this particular occasion from an 'alien' called Ulo, about the perils of plutonium, and that we should mend our ways . . . or else! It was probably – as was suspected at the time – a well-meaning hoax, but the point is that it decisively demonstrates that even among proponents of the ETH there obviously lurked, from almost the very outset, apocalyptic aspirations. Now all this would be almost as hilarious as most of the media have portrayed it down the years – except for the fact that there is strongly circumstantial evidence to indicate that it was the phenomenon itself that initiated, then maintained over the millennia, eschatological expectations. Thereby, it has attempted to 'control' human populations by cynically manipulating, with its various impostures, whatever crackpot apocalyptic cosmologies and ego-driven eschatological delusions the mentally mediocre masses were susceptible to at any given time. That such attempts have increased in number, diversity and frequency since the middle 1800s when, synchronistically, there was an inexplicable upsurge in lunar transient phenomena is perhaps indicative of their real origins.

My own personal experience of this apocalyptic aspect of ufology commenced in the middle 1960s when, by virtue of experimentation with a ouija-board, I eventually became the target of an entity that initially claimed to be the shade of Nerfertiti. At the time I was impressed by the content of *Final Secret of the Illumnati* by Robert Anton Wilson, thus I experimented along the lines indicated in it. The result was that, over a period of months, my home apparently came under seige by the so-called supernatural. Entities, apportations, automatic writing and other 'paranormalities' occurred on the inside. While overhead outside, upsetting my neighbour on one occasion I might add, flew flying saucers of every conceivable kind. By my deliberately 'believing' (it wasn't easy) in a series of 'tunnel realities', sacred and secular, the 'phenomenon' was apparently persuaded to 'tailor' sequentially its appearances to accommodate a number of mutually exclusive frames of reference. Consequently, I experimented in turn mediumistic, miraculous, extraterrestrial and, finally, demonic 'effects', the sole purpose of which seemed to be to 'reinforce' whatever belief system I was currently professing in order that the communicating 'entity' could then involve me in a 'save the world' scenario by implying that I was 'specially chosen' by God, the BVM, advanced aliens or the dear departed because of my inherent intellectual excellence in subscribing to whatever set of beliefs I was currently professing. A somewhat circular strategy I have to admit but, what the hell, this is ufology after all. Fortunately I have not now, and did not have at that time, any delusions about my own intrinsic individual worth, so these essentially ego-inflationary entreaties fell on deaf ears. Eventually, the 'contact' petered out, but it lasted long enough for me to come to the conclusion that the prime qualification for a contactee is a predisposition to the kind of personal delusions of grandeur that allows one to believe that 'superior' entities – of any sort – would 'choose' uninfluential nonentities to alert the human race to the imminence of global apocalypse in preference to the kind of individual and/or institution that has the influence and resources to effectively alert the population. That entities of all kinds do seem predisposed to 'abduct' or 'contact' the more cosmologically credulous individuals in our society strongly indicates that the object of the exercise is deception instead of enlightenment. But if that is the case, what does the communicating life form hope to gain from such deception? Probably exactly what has already been achieved: the creation and maintenance of a specifically eschatological mythology that has allowed it increasingly to 'control' the human race by proxy, while laying the foundations for an overt and uncontested take over at some future date. It has to be suspected from the growing trends in world events that the intelligent dinosaur that was our creator might just be ready to make its attempts to reclaim its property, at which time, in the words of the 'King of the World' *circa* 1890 'the peoples of Agharti will come up from their subterranean caverns to the surface of the earth'.[27]

I think I would prefer the end of the world.

References

[1] *Gods of Aquarius*, Brad Steiger (Panther, 1977).

[2] ibid.

[3] ibid.

[4] Dr Puharich's UFO Fantasies', D. Scott Rogo in *the Amazing Uri Geller*, ed. Martin Ebon (Signet, 1975).

[5] *The Ufonauts*, Hans Holzer (Panther, 1979).

[6] ibid.

[7] *Briefing for the Landing on Planet Earth*, Stuart Holroyd (Corgi, 1979).

[8] Holzer, op. cit.

[9] Holroyd, op. cit.

[10] ibid.

[11] *UFOs: The Final Answer?*, ed. David Barclay and Therese Marie Barclay (Blandford, 1993).

[12] 'Alien Abduction on Ilkley Moor', Peter Hough, *UFO Universe*, 1988.

[13] ibid.

[14] *Aliens Above, Always*, John Magor (Hancock House, 1983).
[15] ibid.
[16] *U.F.O. Abductions*, ed. D. Scott Rogo (Signet, 1980).
[17] ibid.
[10] ibid.
[19] ibid.
[20] ibid.
[21] inid.
[22] *The Andreasson Affair*, Raymond E. Fowler (Bantam, 1980).
[23] *Alien Contact*, Jenny Randles and Paul Whetnall (Neville Spearman, 1984).
[24] ibid.
[25] ibid.
[26] ibid.
[27] *The Lost World Of Agharti*, Alec Maclellan (Souvenir Press, 1982).

CHAPTER 11

Past Masters?

ONE explanation of the UFO phenomenon, and one aimed particularly at the unexpected familiarity with Earth-orientated eschatology of the alleged entities involved in it, is that UFOs and their presumed pilots are voyagers from the future of planet Earth itself. Why the future? Because, according to conventional wisdom, such a solution would adequately explain the recognizably 'advanced' technology, and the appearance of the large-headed, feeble-bodied 'aliens', because both of these seem to conform to popular ideas on the 'laws' of technological and physical 'evolution'. In effect, the TTH (time traveller hypothesis) 'attempts to account for the variation in physical apearance of UFO Occupants by citing the possible evolution of our descendants into various humanoid forms'.[1]

The TTH argues that, in the UFO phenomenon, what we are interfacing with is ourselves from further down the evolutionary road. But, this probability must take into account the problems posed by the possibility of paradox. To alter the past in such a way to modify, or negate completely, a future event, all that might have to happen is that an almost indetectable cause would occur at the correct moment in time in advance of the event that was 'changed' or 'annulled'. In which case, it could be that the past, and even the present, is well packed with paradoxes which cannot ever be identified, simply because a paradox is only a paradox in relation to the future event it modifies or nullifies. To be able to recognize what events are or are not potentially paradoxical, it would be necessary to know the precise future event(s) which are to be modified or negated entirely. This is something of a paradoxical proposition in itself, but one which, if it ever becomes properly understood, might help to explain the known failure rate of UFO prophecy. The trouble is that it also makes it impossible to tell if time travel – in the Wellsian sense – is possible or not. Logically, the past must already contain everything that has happened in the past – even up to and including any temporal tampering from the future that may or may not have occurred. Therefore, although it is tempting to interpret the UFO phenomenon in terms of 'time travellers' from the future, the paradox is that for all practical purposes this interpretation is impossible to verify – even if it is true. This really does nothing to help ufological exegesis when it is faced by some of the statements, and actions, attributed by witnesses to the 'ufonauts' they claim to have encountered, that strongly indicate that 'alien' ideas on conventional chronology could differ radically from these presently subscribed to by humankind. It does not explain, for instance, the ufonaut who, after asking the time of day and being told by the percipient that it was 14.30, countered by saying, 'You lie, it is 4 o'clock.'[2] Or, why:

> In an even more remarkable case in South America, a man who found himself inside a UFO could see the 'pilots' consulting a device contained in a box. He managed to look into this box and saw what looked like a clock, but the clock had no hands.[3]

In the genre the inherent importance of this kind of experience has been 'interpreted' by various 'experts' as being on a par with metaphysical mysticism, or perhaps alchemical obfuscation. This, in effect, implies that such statements and/or experiences contain 'hidden' messages of cosmological momentousness (the 'meaning' of which is modified according to the beliefs of whatever 'expert' is doing the interpreting). But surely this cannot be applied to those incidents where nonsense was apparently indulged in by the communicating entity? As in the case of 'Spectra' who, according to Uri Geller, used a 'distance' measurement as a 'time' measurement by saying it was 'light years in the future'. Or as in the case of Mrs Elissah of Hull, England, who, during the 1970s allegedly 'channelled' the following from an 'alien':

> 'Time' is always against you. In my world this is not so, there is no time as such, our existence goes on, 'we' re-establish ourselves and can therefore continue with what has been placed

before. A strange concept? perhaps, but to us we know no other, you see 'we' are 'THE TIME BENDERS', the Prophets of years to come, and of long since past. Once 'Masters' of the World, now the inhabitants of a planet as different from yours as could be imagined.[4]

But, unless 'aliens' of all sorts are being deliberately deceptive, might we be missing the point by assuming that what is nonsensical to us is equally nonsensical to the communicating intelligence? Perhaps, with good reason, their conceptualization does include 'light years' as a measurement of time, and/or 'time bending' as a feasible technology. Perhaps they are indeed time travellers, but – as with the rest of us – they have moved from the past forward, rather than from the future backwards.

As far as it is possible to tell, time travel is a one-way street from past to future. For most of us this means moving in time at a pedestrian 60 seconds to the minute by 'surfing' on the crest of the time wave that we know as 'now'. However, the speed at which you travel in the direction of the future is modifiable, in that the faster you move through space, the slower you move through time (which I am sure is indicative of something profound in the relationship between time and space). This effect is called 'time dilation' (rather than 'space compression' which is equally accurate), and the fact that it is an objectively real effect might have staggering ramifications for UFOs and the beings who, apparently, operate them. In fact, time travel utilizing 'time dilation' could adequately explain how both we, and a certain other dinosaur derivative, were able successfully to survive the Cretaceous cataclysm that wiped out the phylum that gave rise to us both. Apparently, as far as can be ascertained by scientific hindsight, the conditions at the close of the Cretaceous coincidentally conformed to those of a nuclear winter, as discussed earlier. This, when taken in conjunction with the plethora of global folklore that deals in concepts like 'Ragnarok', 'Armageddon', and the 'War in Heaven', is circumstantial enough to make one wonder if those 'end of the world' scenarios so beloved of all manner of so-called 'supernatural' beings are based more in their experiences in the past than in any foreknowledge they might have of the future? This is a train of thought that leads inevitably to the speculation that the ecological disaster at the close of the Cretaceous period might not have been a natural calamity at all.

So what could have really happened? Is it possible that the Biblical 'war in heaven' has a basis in fact after all? Given the existence of a pre-Cretaceous civilization on a par with or, more probably, superior to the present one – and therefore more than capable of the kind of conflict that would produce the conditions indicated in the fossil record – we can safely assume that it would also have had means of survival. Underground shelters? Certainly. Installations on the Moon? Probably. A colony on Mars? Possibly. But the most interesting class of survivors would be the inadvertent ones, those individuals who could have been engaged in deep space exploration and whose eventual return to the solar system would be subject to 'time dilation' brought about by the velocities necessary to enable their interstellar explorations . . . but more of them later.

At this remove in time, it is impossible to be absolutely certain of the precise planetary conditions prior to the Cretaceous ecocrash. Whatever they were, they had had (at least) a 150-million-year period of continuity in which to develop. So, given a needle of truth in a haystack of mythology, it seems not outside the bounds of probability that a civilization far more technologically advanced than the present one might have met its end when the dinosaurs died. The problem is not so much proving it as in persuading the professional palaeontological pundits to accept the undeniable import of the evidence contained in global mythologies and what are sometimes referred to as OOPARTS (out of place artefacts). In this respect, there might be none so blind as those who preconceive by assuming that the human race is the first and only expression of biointelligence this planet has ever produced. The difficulties inherent in arguing for a global civilization in antiquity, similar to the present one, are almost insurmountable. This is not because there is any lack of evidence, but because palaeontological preconceptions generated by Victorian 'scientific' atheism are particularly persistent, while religious fanaticism remains as intransigent as ever. So, from whatever angle the subject is approached, the barricades of bigotry are erected in defence of prevailing anthropomorphic preconceptions – sacred or secular. However, once it is accepted that the human race might not be either the first, last, best, or only expression of biointelligence produced by planet Earth, the way is opened to a wider interpretation of extant anthropological anomalies and

palaeontological puzzles, like the existence of obviously manufactured objects in strata several millions of years old, supposedly
from well before any civilization capable of manufacturing
anything came into being: for example, the 'cube', discovered by
Dr Gurlt in 1886 in a German coal mine, which had been
embedded in a layer dating from the Tertiary period. It was at
least tens of millions of years old and probably from the period
immediately succeeding that which saw the (still unexplained)
demise of the dinosaurs:

> Some specialists of that period, including Dr Gurlt himself,
> said it was a fossil meteorite. Others declared it a meteorite that
> had been reworked . . . Finally, still other experts said that the
> objects was manufactured.[5]

Surely 'experts' should be able to tell if an object is manufactured
or not? How about you? If you found a cube made of hard carbon/
nickel steel with an incision running around the middle of it and
with two opposing faces slightly rounded, what would you make
of it? And if you found it in a piece of coal dating from the days
of the dinosaurs, what then? If you subscribed to the dogmatisms
of old time religion (Biblical fundamentalism), or new time
religion (scientific fundamentalism), your impartiality would be
eroded by your need to uphold your 'beliefs', and an obviously
manufactured object might become a 'meteorite'. It is this need to
accommodate anthropomorphic orthodoxies that has called into
being the insupportible 'ancient astronaut' theories to account for
archaeological anomalies that are better explained by admitting
the technological civilization is not unique to either the present
day, or to humankind.

To finite creatures such as us, a million years is a long, long
time, but in the chronology of the cosmos it is little more than an
eye blink. Even 70 million years, to us an incomprehensible time
span, is only slighter longer than a summer's day . . . or, perhaps
more pertinently, the passing of a nuclear winter. If our present
civilization were to perish permanently, I dare to suggest that 70
million years later there would be little trace of our technology
left, and the descendants of any physical survivors would no
doubt end up deluding themselves that they were either 'created'
by 'God', or the pinnacle of an impartial process called
'evolution'. They would become so infuriated by any attempt to

indicate otherwise that they would ignore any and all evidence that tended to point towards other, less ego-inflating, solutions about their origins; just as we probably have. Looked at from our present cultural perspective, folklore/mythology should be suspected of being a method for transmitting the truth about certain things that, at the time the folklore/mythology was becoming part of 'human culture', were deemed either 'miraculous' or 'magical' – two concepts we should have now almost entirely dispensed with in the face of our escalating technological expertise. It should now seem probable that all folklore/ mythology – and in this category must be included the Bible – depends on fanciful descriptions derived from facts that the raconteur could not comprehend. For instance, should we disappear from the world stage, as did the dinosaurs, what would those left to pick up the pieces make of the facts of our vanished technology that, eventually (inevitably as generation succeeded generation), they only knew from garbled descriptions in tales of wonder (i.e., folklore/mythology)? In all probability, they would do what we presently should not be doing: confusing folklore/ mythology with fiction instead of recognizing it as fact expressed poetically. I admit that it is all too easy to hypothesize (one way and another ufologists have been doing it for years), because the data can be made to support any contention, depending on which portion is accepted as relevant. Any truly tenable hypothesis must be inclusive of everything, and by this means also provide a holistic interpretation of what UFO evidence there is in such a way as to reconcile the seemingly irreconcilable aspects of 'nuts and bolts' ufology, 'psychic' saucery, and sundry other apparently mutually exclusive paradigms. At the same time, it should adequately explain why the global power élite might have considered it necessary to withhold from the public the solution to the mystery that they had known since, at the very latest, 1960. Instead, it prefers to weather the slings and arrows of ufologists incensed by not having their particular paradigm 'officially' admitted by any Establishment. Such an inclusive 'hypothesis' would also have to take into account that, throughout the 'modern' UFO era, Establishment denials have stressed that UFOs have no defence significance, that no extraterrestrials were being kept on ice in Hangar 18, and that there is no evidence indicating that UFOs are extraterrestrial vehicles. All of which must be accepted as possibly containing more than an element of truth, but which can be suspected of being carefully couched in such terms as to encourage conclusion-jumping in entirely the wrong direction. The 'Return of the Dinosaurs' hypothesis does all this . . . and more!

By laying to one side the human chauvinisms that blind us to other, equally plausible, interpretations of the discoveries of palaeontology, we can admit (if only for the sake of argument) that the Cretaceous catastrophe could just as easily have been caused by a nuclear war as by a cometary impact. In fact, this event is now so far in the past that scientific insistence on 'rational' explanations for its onset must be suspect, especially when it is realized that for some 200 years this same science 'rationally' explained the phenomenon of 'ball lightning' 'as being caused by screech owls which, having spent time in the hollow of a rotten tree, had become coated with a phosphorescent material'.[6] This explanation was achieved by scientific presumption ignoring those reported aspects of ball lightning which did not conform to prevailing scientific preconceptions. So this absurd explanation was apparently 'rational' enough to 'satisfy scientific circles until 1965 – in other words for two centuries'.[7]

I am sure readers will know of similar examples of demonstrable (and unfortunately ongoing) 'scientific' shortsightedness, so I will labour the point no further. Instead I will proceed to re-interpret accepted data (scientific, theological and ufological) in light of my proposed 'Return of the Dinosaurs' hypothesis. Because the time span to be dealt with is so incomprehensibly long, at least to us, I make no claims to absolute accuracy. However I am content to point out initially that something certainly survived the Cretaceous catastrophe, otherwise I would not be here typing these words. Any who survived must have been traumatized to a degree inconceivable even to us who now possess the means to repeat history – or as in this case, prehistory. Because of this trauma-tization, plus the ongoing effects of residual radiation, and the other deleterious bequests of nuclear war (some of which I am certain even we are unaware of), recovery must have been a slow and painful process, the precise details of which may never be known. However, it is probably not entirely inaccurate to say that in the centuries immediately after the disaster, radiation-modified mutations ruled the surface of the planet. Below them, survivors of the erstwhile dominant species (intelligent dinosaur) cowered in caverns, wondering if they would ever see the light of day again.

As every reader must realize, it is impossible to document definitively the precise progress of humankind from beyond the radioactive remains of a prehistoric civilization to the present day. However, there are hints, pointing to the possibility that, due to the anthropomorphic intransigence of modern science, 'An immense error has warped our understanding of our genesis, and history and prehistory have been distorted at will.'[8] Despite the conventional consensus, there is still no irrefutable 'rational' explanation for when the city of Tiahuanaco, the platform at Baalbek, and even the Sphinx and Pyramids at Gizeh, came into existence. Also, modern science cannot explain, or even convincingly explain away, the existence of out-of-place artefacts, such as the previously mentioned German 'cube'. Or, even more indicative of an ancient civilization, the 'objet d'art' blown out of seemingly solid rock on Meeting House Hill, Dorchester, Massachusetts, reported in the June 1951 issue of *Scientific American*. That this particular artefact was manufactured is beyond question. It was a vase, 4½ in (11 cm) tall, which had designs, inlaid in silver, on its sides. Once again, the strata from which it was recovered indicated it to be several million years old. Even so, and despite the number of OOPARTS in existence, scientists doggedly cling to their preconceptions, ignoring every discovery which does not fit into their theories regarding the 'evolutionary' genesis and development of humankind on Earth. This explanatory vacuum has been filled by those who argue that such artefacts 'prove' the existence of ancient astronauts. However, as all these OOPARTS are manufactured from materials readily available on Earth, and which conform to manufacturing parameters recognizable to our technological culture, it would seem that:

> A closer look at the strange artefacts now suggests that OOPARTS originated in a man-made civilization – one that antedated known history – one that attained an elevated degree of development, but was destroyed to such an extent by a devastating catastrophe in the distant past that only a few remnants of its science and technology survived among the inferior cultures that succeeded it.[9]

Further indications that a technological civilization existed in the prehistoric past can be gleaned from folklore and mythology. They can be gleaned not just from the Bible, which is a fairly recent cosmological compilation, but from those works which are known to pre-date it by a considerable period and which are thought to originate in an earlier, verbal, tradition. Even as late as 50 years ago, the descriptions of advanced technology contained in works like the *Mahabharata* were considered fantastical, but now:

> Seen in the light of the latter twentieth century there is much fact and very little fable in these stark accounts of a sophisticated weaponry, all too horribly like our own.[10]

This strengthens the speculation that the conventional consensus regarding the progress of life on Earth is seriously flawed by its inability to come to terms with this increasing accuracy in ancient accounts. To be fair, though, it has to be admitted, 'Modern Science and conventional thinking are not so much wrong – although in some areas they are seriously wrong – as incomplete.'[11] In other words, they seem to be unable to come to terms with the fact that

> It is demonstrable from many sources that the phenomenon that has come to be known in this latter half of the twentieth century as 'UFOs' has been endemic throughout history, and probably even before that. In some way yet to be determined, it can only be that the UFO Phenomenon has an interface with human society as it developed on this planet.[12]

Although the presence of the UFO phenomenon in prehistorical times can be deduced from extant evidence, the really interesting correlations only commence with the Biblical account of the beginnings of Jewry. According to this, some 6,000 years ago a seemingly superior non-human life form attempted to segregate a specific segment of the human family from the rest, probably to achieve domination by proxy of the human race as a whole. The attempt apparently failed, as have other similar attempts (i.e., Paulianity, Mormonism, spiritualism, Aetherius Society, Raelianism) by this same non-human life form throughout recorded history. However, you could be right if you see these ongoing attempts as a means to dissipate human energies into unproductive conflicts about nonsensical and non-existent issues not entirely unconnected to the delusion that 'God' (or the 'superior' personage of your choice) takes sides.

The apparent alien intervention in human affairs is accurately recorded, if inexactly attributed, in the Biblical accounts dealing with the alleged appearances of 'God' to various Old Testament prophets (i.e., Moses, Ezekiel, etc.). Such contacts continued, sporadically, until, in the latter half of the nineteenth century, the format changed, and the tempo quickened. That this change followed the sudden escalation of Lunar Transient Phenomena reported in 1869 has to be suspected of being indicative that something significant had taken place. What if that significant event was the return of interstellar explorers to a lunar 'base' that had been inactive or operating on 'autopilot' for 70 million years. They would have soon discovered that the global civilization that they had left when embarking on their flight was gone, and that the planet was in the hands of the apparent descendants of a life form that they had themselves bred as a bio-servomechanism. They would probably have already found the base on Mars uninhabited before going on to the Moon and so, finding the Moon also uninhabited (except perhaps for mechanical maintenance and repair robots), they would have wanted to learn if any of their kind had survived on the home planet, Earth. Hence the outbreak of coherent, transient lunar phenomena in the form of geometric light formations. At the time, human scientists suspected that these lunar lights might be 'messages' of some kind, but erroneously assumed that if they were they *had* to be directed at humankind. More probably, they were seen and acknowledged by those they were actually aimed at. Having established that some of their own kind had survived on Earth, the next task facing the returned interstellar explorers would have been to make a landing on Earth itself. Something – if the ramifications of the Siberian sky crash of 1908 were anything to go by – was initially easier said than done. Whatever, it is a matter of public record that on 30 June 1908, an object, which had 'coincidentally' used the same 're-entry corridor' utilized some 60 years later by returning American Moonshots, eventually ended up by exploding at an altitude of 5 miles (8 km) above the sparsely populated Siberian plateau known as the Tunguska. Throughout its descent, this object behaved in a way that was completely at odds with what would have been expected of an incoming inanimate 'bolide':

> Therefore, although conventional science would feel less threatened by an inanimate explanation for it, on the lines of meteor, comet, small black hole, or even contra-terrene matter, the recorded behaviour of the object makes 'intelligently guided device' the most probable explanation.[13]

If the Tunguska event was a failed attempt at landing, then the sequel, some five years later, seems to have been more successful. Initially spotted by amateur astronomers, and more casual and less qualified observers, the objects which entered our atmosphere on the night of 9 February 1913 were eventually observed by professionals of the calibre of Professor Chant of Toronto University. Apparently, the objects were flying low enough to cause sonic 'booms', but despite this immersion in our atmosphere they were apparently able to leave it again, because, on this occasion, nothing apparently 'crashed'. Although, yet again, the astronomical community would prefer to label these objects as 'meteors', the extant evidence seems to indicate that 'an extra-terrestrial operation that failed disastrously in 1908 succeeded in 1913'.[14] That something unusual occurred is attested to by the fact that from then on the phenomenon of UFOs began to proliferate and diversify. There was the 'dancing sun' (daylight disc) of Fatima in 1917, followed in 1926 by the Roerich expedition's sighting of a 'huge spheroid body' (i.e., daylight disc) in western China. Here, powerful field-glasses were used by Nicholas Roerich and his European companions to view the object. Then came the 'Foo-fighters' of World War 2, seen and reported by pilots in every theatre of war, and the 'ghost rockets' of the middle 1940s, seen and reported (and on many occasions photographed) by any number of witnesses. Finally, there is the UFO phenomenon, as it is known today, a phenomenon attested to by millions, but still ignored by science. If these intrusions are interpreted as extraterrestrial vehicles of various kinds, it seems to predicate that the Earth is being visited by representatives of every civilization in the known Universe which has a space-exploration capability. Is the Earth really that interesting?

Probably not. The ETH is made even more untenable as an explanation if we try to account for the various 'alien' life forms that have been reported by alleging that these too are all extraterrestrials. Statistically speaking, it is highly improbable that the vast majority of these should be so unbelievably humanoid, have no obvious difficulty in breathing our atmosphere and – perhaps the most incredible of all – subscribe to our parochial belief systems if they indeed had a multiplicity of planetary origins. However, if we accept the proposition that the UFO phenomenon is native to the Earth and is humankind's interface with the life form that brought it into being, then many explanatory difficulties are rendered redundant and we can begin to unravel the tangled web that ufology has become over these past 40-plus years.

A tentative timetable for explaining the UFO phenomenon in terms of the survival on Earth of an intelligent dinosaur type, and the eventual numerical augmentation and technological renaissance triggered by the return of interstellar explorers, might be expected to go something like this. Firstly, the low level, but consistently pervasive, presence of 'something' non-human during prehistory can be put down to the activities of those dinosaur individuals who had survived on Earth and who operated from 'hidden' bases that came to be known as Shangri-la, Belovodye, Agharti and Schamballah to the humans surviving on the surface. These 'hidden chiefs', remembering how they once ruled the ecological roost, continually tried to re-establish their dominance of humankind at regular intervals by attempting to play upon our (probably genetically implanted or enhanced by them) apparent need to 'worship'. By deliberately posing as 'gods', our erstwhile masters pursued a strategy to re-educate their creature in blind submission to their will. In the guise of such creatures as the 'Oannes' of the Babylonians and, perhaps more significantly, the 'Nommo' of the Dogon tribe of Africa, they attempted to regain their control of humankind. The Old Testament is as good a documentation of the initiation and maintenance of this kind of strategy as you are likely to find, especially since there are indications that this particular initiative is still ongoing. That humankind's various belief systems, including ufology, are the result of such initiatives is suggested by the close similarity between the many beliefs of antiquity and those relating to the Judaeo-Christian mythology. This is the kind of similarity exemplified by the Dogon mythology, in which:

> The Nommo dies and is resurrected, acting as a sacrifice for us, to purify and cleanse the Earth. The parallels with Christ are extraordinary, even extending to Nommo being crucified on a tree, and forming a eucharistic meal for humanity and then being resurrected.[15]

To emphasize further the probability that our beliefs have been authored by a single source, one has only to contemplate the puzzle of the 'counterfeit' Christianity that the Conquistadores and their proseletyizing padres found awaiting them in the New World, and the fact, 'Almost everything that has ever been said about Jesus has parallels in ancient Indian legends.'[16] It is curiously coincidental that it is in this very same ancient Indian legendary material that those (only now becoming recognizable as such) descriptions of 'super technology' appear. It would seem a fair assumption that the 'space travel' capability was lost at the time of the Cretaceous cataclysm, so that until interstellar explorers began to return, all operations, including the 'spaceship of Ezekiel', were undertaken with an Earthbound, albeit superior, technology. In all probability, the survivors on Earth were aware of the possible return of interstellar explorers. This, at least in part, was the stimulus for the demonstrably entity-generated folklore concerning 'Judgement Day' or, in more modern terms, a 'mass landing' of UFOs. As I have said before, it is impossible to be precise, because the real situation is likely to have been far more complex than any speculation about it. Truth, for the most part, is nearly always stranger than scientific rationalism would have it be. If you want UFOs to be objectively 'real', and still accommodate the apparent contradictions in the data, then the only option is to explain them in terms of the clandestine operations of an intelligent non-human life form indigenous to the Earth. A life form, the existence of which, for obvious reasons, the ubiquitous 'man in the street' has been deliberately disinformed, misinformed and underinformed by the various 'vested interests' of State and Religion, even though it is odds on that the truth is already known by them. Even so, it is more likely that it is the ufonauts who are the past masters at the art of deception, because they must know that 'Human life is ruled by imagination and myth.'[17] They know this because this was demonstrably their preferred method of 'control' in the days before the 'war in heaven', and a method which they hope will help them stop prehistory from repeating itself. Some hopes if present trends are anything to go by.

References

[1] *The Archetype Experience*, Gregory L. Little (Rainbow Books, 1984).
[2] *UFOs: The Psychic Solution*, Jacques Vallée (Panther Books, 1977).
[3] ibid.
[4] *Portraits of Alien Encounters*, Nigel Watson (Valis Books, 1990).
[5] *Mysteries of the Earth*, Jacques Bergier (Futura, 1974).
[6] ibid.
[7] ibid.
[8] *Legacy of the Gods*, Robert Charroux (Sphere, 1979).
[9] *Secrets of the Lost Races*, René Noorbergen (New English Library, 1978).
[10] *Flying Saucers Have Landed*, D. Leslie and G. Adamski (Futura, 1977).
[11] *Guardians of the Ancient Wisdom*, Stan Gooch (Fontana, 1980).
[12] *UFOs: The Final Answer?*, ed. David Barclay and Therese Marie Barclay (Blandford, 1993).
[13] ibid.
[14] Bergier, op. cit.
[15] *The Sirius Mystery*, Robert K. G. Temple (Futura, 1976).
[16] *Jesus Lived in India*, Holger Kersten (Element Books, 1986).
[17] Vallée, op. cit.

CHAPTER 12
Gimme That Ol' time Religion

A MAJOR stumbling block to any impartial appraisal of evidence indicating alternative explanations for the origins of humankind is our race's regrettable inclination to chauvinism. In this respect, the theory of evolution can be seen as the scientific equivalent of creationism, in that they both subscribe to the notion of the human race as the apex of existence. With anthropomorphic arrogance, we presume to designate ourselves *Homo sapiens sapiens* and condescendingly wonder if there might be other such 'intelligent' life forms in the Universe. Statistically, the odds are that they are intelligent beings in the Universe, but we presently have no grounds for presuming that the human race is necessarily one of them. Despite our ongoing cosmological egomania, it is clear, 'We remain as a curious mixture of the brute and the civilized.'[1] The other life forms who share this planet are able to find their way from the cradle to the grave without apparently needing their equivalent of the fantasies with which we encumber our existence. Without benefit of the pontifications of popes or professors, the absolution of priests or psychiatrists, and the oracles of prophets or pollsters, the other animals on Earth live – and die – in accordance with the laws of nature. Demonstrably, the human race does not, and this alone should be sufficient to indicate some possible unnaturalness in the origin of our species.

Before creationists become overexcited by the apparent trend of the argument in favour of humankind's possible unnatural origins, I must point out that I am not going to advance arguments in favour of an omnipresent, omnipotent 'God' as the guilty party. However, if global mythology is anything to go by, then something almost certainly 'made' us, and probably for purposes far removed from playing harps in some problematical hereafter. According to the myths of the Quiche Maya, those who brought humankind into being deliberated thus: 'let those who are to nourish and sustain us appear, the noble sons, the civilized vassals; let man appear, humanity, on the face of the earth'.[2] Despite the reference to 'noble sons', this clearly puts us in our place. Following on from this, Mayan mythology goes on to describe how the 'first men' were endowed with the ability to 'know all', to see the large and the small in the sky and on Earth, and to examine the round face of the Earth. This is just about what today's technology empowers us to do. From this, it can be suspected that humanity was originally developed as some kind of living servomechanism, genetically engineered to understand and operate our 'masters' technology, which obviously included a global-surveillance facility in all respects similar to the one today. We must have got too good at it, because the myth goes on to tell how our makers became worried and said to themselves:

> Let us check a little their desires, because it is not well what we see. Must they perchance be the equals of ourselves, their Makers, who see afar, who know all and see all?[3]

Uncannily, this echoes the Biblical account of how and why humankind and master parted company – not on the best of terms. To compound this correlation, in the myths of the Dogon the being known as 'Ogo the Fox' seems to represent humankind: 'an imperfect intelligent species who "descended" or originated on this planet'.[4] What makes this mythology so compellingly corroborative is that it supplies the clue to who 'Lucifer' of the Christian tradition really was and so it restores the events surrounding the 'fall' of humankind to the realms of the objectively real. According to Robert Temple:

> It comes as a shock to realize we are Ogo, the imperfect, the meddler, the outcast. Ogo rebelled at his own creation and remained unfinished. He is the equivalent of Lucifer in our own tradition in the Christian West.[5]

The implication is obvious. If Ogo is ourselves *and* the equivalent of Lucifer, then *we* are Lucifer, and a lot of things that were spiritually obscure become materialistically clear. If this Luciferic correlation is correct, it would seem to indicate that it was the human race who, in effect, said 'we will not serve', and so precipitated the 'war in heaven'. In this context, the original 'original sin' can be deduced to have been rebellion rather than sex, and the consequences so dire that for aeons thereafter the survivors of the conflagration sought to hide their own guilt from themselves by succumbing to the racial amnesia brought about by the trauma of the almost terminal conflict the rebellion engendered. To be exact in this matter is impossible due to the timescale involved. However, that something of this nature occurred can be deduced from the facts of our existence. Without doubt we are the most destructive being on the planet. While protesting peace, we go to war. In all areas we seek confrontation and conflict. Even in the abstract we speak of 'conquering' – nature, space, poverty, disease – in fact, almost anything that we see as 'opposing' us. We are the most territorially aggressive species extant. Even when it comes to UFOs, it seems that the most aggravating aspect of their existence is that they refuse to submit themselves to our 'scientific' scrutiny. We want what we think they have got. At some psychological level, we seem to want them to 'attack' us in the fashion of *Earth Vs The Flying Saucers*, for then they would be playing the game according to rules we understand and excel at; that they haven't, probably indicates that the Establishment is quite correct when it says that UFOs have no defence significance. In the military sense it is probable that, in the UFO phenomenon, we are not facing an imminent invasion by an exterior enemy, but an ongoing attempt by a superior indigenous life form to reclaim the planet and re-establish itself as the dominant species without provoking the human race into repeating prehistory. Just as Jacques Vallée has speculated, the UFO phenomenon is trying to control (or more accurately, in my opinion, trying to regain control of) humankind. But contrary to his assumption that in the machinations of the UFO phenomenon 'we are dealing with the next form of religion.[6] I think it is more likely that the phenomenon is trying to re-establish the oldest form of 'religion' on earth: humankind's unquestioning subservience to themselves. In this endeavour they have consistently 'chosen' ego-driven individuals and through them tried to manipulate humanity as a whole. In the past, they claimed to be God, and the BVM, allowed themselves to be taken

for 'angels' and 'discarnate' souls. Then, probably when their
compatriots returned from their stellar wanderings some time
towards the end of the 1800s, they began to update their 'image'
to 'superior alien', in keeping with humankind's burgeoning
scientifiction expectations. Perhaps at Fatima they began their
final attempt to control humankind 'religiously'. If so, the
'dancing sun', advertised in advance as a 'miracle' so big *all*
would believe, failed. The plague, the so-called Spanish flu
epidemic of 1918 that was seeded during the 'apparitions', also
failed to reduce the human race to manageable (to them)
proportions. This is probably why World War 2 was not won by
their probable protégé, the dictator Adolf Hitler. The war was
threatened by the BVM at Fatima if the human race did not
'repent', so it arguably was an integral part of the plan to control
the human race. Had Hitler won, I am certain that the 'secret of
Fatima' would have been revealed in 1960 as instructed. Instead,
'The appointed day came, the appointed day went, and nothing,
an unbelievable nothing, issues from the Vatican.'[7]

The decision not to reveal the contents of the 'secret' in order
to 'preserve the mystery' caused the Catholic Church an
irreversible 'loss of face', just as the denial of the existence of
UFOs has caused the various Establishments endless embarrass-
ments. To begin to suspect that the 'secret of Fatima' could be the
same as the 'secret of the saucers', one only has to ask why two of
the most powerful vested interests on this planet would rather
endure ongoing ridicule than reveal those secrets.

Is such censorship, and denial, necessary because – despite the
ufological suspicions regarding 'advanced technology' – the most
potent weapon in the 'alien' armoury is not some planet smashing
'death star' but just the plain unvarnished truth? Truth so
devastatingly detrimental to one particular human delusion that it
is probable that not just the scientists Morris Jessup, Wilhelm
Reich and many others, some known, some unknown, have died
in pursuit of it, but possibly the lives of presidents and popes have
been sacrificed to 'preserve the mystery'. To give substance to the
suspicion that UFOs represent the late twentieth-century's
experience of what other less secular generations (encouraged by
the phenomenon) would have called 'God', we can begin by
comparing what allegedly happened during the crucifixion to
what actually happened during the penultimate visit of the BVM

to Fatima. Christian tradition holds that at the crucifixion of Christ, the sun was darkened. This biblical phenomenon has been explained by atheist and agnostic as being a probable coincidental (another scientific 'miracle'?) 'eclipse'. However, it could just as easily have been caused by something else. On 13 September 1917, at the beginning of the penultimate 'apparition' at Fatima:

> The sun's light was peculiarly dimmed, even though it was shining in a sky devoid of clouds. This time it dimmed to such an extent that, according to eyewitness reports: 'The stars became visible.'[8]

If similar effects imply similar causes, then we can only suspect that whatever caused the dimming of the sun at the crucifixion was present at Fatima, and wonder why 'religion' has had such a strong and ongoing affinity with the kind of manifestation that, these days, is believed by millions (encouraged by the phenomenon) to be attributable to UFO 'technology'. The recognition of this UFO–religion correlation is crucial not only to the proper understanding of what the UFO phenomenon is, but also to why the various world Establishments (military, civil, scientific and theological) could never willingly admit to knowing the real truth about the UFO phenomenon well in advance of the alleged report made by Kenneth Arnold in 1947. Although Establishment-generated ufolore tries to stress the 1947 'genesis' of flying saucery, it is possible to demonstrate that, well before that date, Adolf Hitler was in actual contact with the entities we now know as EBEs, and was probably operating under their direct guidance. From many sources, not the least of which is *Hitler's Secret Sciences* by Nigel Pennick, it is incontrovertibly indicated that Nazism was a religion rather than a political party. There is evidence to suggest that the Third Reich was based on the occult belief that the novel *The Coming Race* by George Bulwer Lytton was factual. It now seems possible that:

> The belief in *The Coming Race* as a factual document was passed down to Hitler via a chain of 'Black' Occultists, themselves steeped in the original traditions regarding a hidden kingdom called Agharti or Schamballah, and who believed themselves to be in communication with the 'Secret Chiefs' who dwelt in such places.[9]

Certainly, it is on record that as early as 1936, under the direct supervision of Himmler, the Nazi search for the 'hidden kingdom' was in full swing. Can it be possible that they found what they were looking for, did a deal with its inhabitants, and launched World War 2 on the strength of it? Whatever the truth of the matter, it was in 1938 that a Nazi experiment with 'high energy' transmitters produced a side-effect which was to become more familiar many years later in ufolore. Apparently two 'transmitters' were erected, on the Brocken (a peak famed for the 'Brocken Spectre', a well known and understood optical effect) and on the peak of Feldburg, near Frankfurt. When this futuristic apparatus was in operation, 'There were soon reports of strange phenomena in the vicinity of the Brocken tower. Cars travelling along the mountain roads would suddenly have engine failure.'[10] Once again, if similar effects imply similar causes, there is every reason to suppose that in 1938 Nazi Germany was experimenting with the technology that caused the 'car paralysis' phenomenon now inextricably linked with the UFO phenomenon. With this in mind it is as well to remember that Nazi technology is also credited with:

the invention of the world's first flying jet aircraft, nerve gasses, TV-guided missiles, rocket planes thirty years ahead of their time, and ballistic missiles which formed the basis for the postwar space programmes of both the USA and USSR.[11]

How was such techno prowess attained by a 'political' system apparently steeped in 'occult' superstitions. The answer – probably from contact with whoever gave them the rudiments of the technology to cause 'engine failure' – is unsettling. So when it is realized that these innovations were probably intended to give Nazism the victory and bring about a 'new world order' in which humankind would be ruled by the 'master race' (which the Nazis, albeit erroneously, thought would be themselves), the Nazi adventure becomes more than just another historical aberration. That Nazi Germany was 'contacteeism' taken to its ultimate is argued by the incredible animosity the system had towards the original 'chosen race', the Jews, and its almost equal animosity towards the offshoot of Judaism, Christianity, in particular Roman Catholicism. These almost inexplicable animosities (considering Hitler was born, and died, a Roman Catholic) find their echo in much of the 'contactee' culture of the UFO age, especially that which seeks to transmute the biblical Jesus into 'Sananda', a kind of Aryan 'Cosmic Christ', whose 'channelled' words are often at odds with the message of the Christian Gospel. Is it more than mere coincidence that much of what is now accepted in UFO-related New Age thinking was anticipated by Adolf Hitler who, more than once, apparently told his closest minions that:

> The world has reached a turning point; we are now at a critical moment in time . . . The planet will undergo an upheaval which you uninitiated people cannot understand.[12]

Such a statement would be at home in the ramblings of many a modern UFO 'contactee', as would Hitler's obsession with an ill-defined 'evolution' of the human race, by some kind of biological selection, into a creature half man and half god. If further proof were needed that Hitler was a 'contactee', there was the incident at his 'Eagle's Eyrie' in the Bavarian mountains, when he was discovered 'in his room looking wildly about him. "He! He! He's been here!" he gasped.'[13] Hitler apparently did not expand on that description, but his reported condition when found is reminiscent of that which afflicts UFO abductees. Disassociation, sensory deprivation and visual hallucination. At one point he apparently cried out, 'There, there! In the corner! Who's that?'[14] Those with him could see nothing unusual, and eventually they persuaded the obviously terrified Hitler that nobody was there. But this might have been because whoever was there, and whom only Hitler could see (an entity accomplishment noted at Fatima, and more recently in UFO-entity appearances), had gone. One final element in the Nazi puzzle that unerringly points to 'entity' involvement is the persistent rumour that a group of 'Tibetans' existed in Berlin who were all killed when that city was taken by the Allies. It is alleged, 'When the Russians entered Berlin, they found among the corpses a thousand volunteers for death in German uniform, without any papers or badges, of Himalayan origin.'[15] Is it possible that they were not 'Tibetans' at all, but that this was a cover story to explain the existence in Berlin of the bodies of several, small, vaguely oriental-looking entities? If so, it would not be the first, nor the last, time UFO entities were taken for orientals. For instance, on or about 25 April 1897, during the course of the 'mystery airship' flap in the USA, a Judge L.A. Burn came upon a strange-looking object in McKinney Bayou, Texarkana, Arkansas, which he took to be the 'airship' about which the papers had recently been full. He told a reporter from the *Daily Texarkanian*, 'It was manned by three men who spoke a foreign language, but judging from their looks, would take them to be Japs.'[16] Is it not possible, then, that at the end of World War 2 similar entities were taken to be Tibetans? Or perhaps this 'identification' was given because the 'UFO cover-up' was even then in operation because, according to John A. Keel, 'It is probable that some small group within the U.S. government first began to suspect the truth about UFOs during World War II.'[17] Such suspicions, which I feel must have existed in some quarters even before the outbreak of World War 2, will have been fuelled by rumours that Hitler was in contact with a mysterious group known as 'The Society of Green Men', a representative of whom, apparently code-named 'the man with the green gloves' 'was regularly visited by Hitler. He was said by the Initiates to "possess the keys to the Kingdom of Agharti".'[18] This is tantamount to saying that this possible LGM and his group were connected to the lands inside the Earth, and therefore were probably members of the remnant of 'intelligent' dinosaurs which had taken refuge therein at the time of the Cretaceous calamity. Such allegations must be looked at in conjunction with the Nazi connection to the events at Fatima, their outlandish racial ideas, their sudden technological 'spurt', and the upsurge in UFO sightings which occurred during the war, especially during its closing stages, and which has gone on unabated ever since. All of this makes it seem not outside the bounds of probability that the Nazi adventure was another attempt by the intelligence behind the UFO phenomenon to impose a 'religion' on humankind that would enable it to regain control of a population which it regarded as a dangerously malfunctioning bioelectric-servomechanism. If this is so, then the question to ask to solve the secret of the saucers is: do malfunctioning servomechamisms have immortal souls?

The possibility that the answer might be 'no' is likely to be what has sustained the global power élite in its determination to disinform the general populace about UFOs, until such times as it could come up with a way to defuse the sociological dynamite inherent in that answer. Nobody wants to be first in telling the human race that the flying saucers and are real and Earthbased, and that we are their occupants' servants. The truth of the latter has been staring us in the face all along, but as there are none so blind as those who preconceive, we have ignored all those clues which made it quite plain that, as the indefatigable anomaly-researcher Charles Hoy Fort perspicaciously pointed out, 'We are property.'[19] Even the Bible clearly indicates that we were made to be a slave in perpetuity to our 'breeder'. Equally, all the mythological evidence indicates that the creature (the intelligent dinosaur?) which 'created' (i.e., bred) us to serve its purposes exclusively really had no, nor yet has any, conception of the existence of such things as 'human rights'. In support of this contention, we only have to look to the reported behaviour of the so-called 'alien abductors' towards those they snatch and seemingly experiment upon. On no occasion has it been reported that the entities asked the permission of the abductee before carrying out what are, quite recognizably, invasive medical procedures upon them. The experience of Whitley Strieber in this regard is enough to put beyond reasonable doubt the UFO phenomenon's attitude towards the human race. Understandably upset by the impersonal and casually cruel treatment he received at the hands of his 'visitors', he protested, '. . . "You have no right".'[20] His abductor's reply was breathtaking in its assumption of authority. According to Strieber he was told, '"We do have a right." Five enormous words. Stunning words. *We do have a right*. Who gave it to them? By what progress of ethics had they arrived at that conclusion?'[21] Apparently Whitley Strieber was unable to comprehend the full ramifications of that reply as applied to the status of the human race in the eyes of those who operate behind the UFO phenomenon. Strange really, when it is realized that he had to have recourse to the 'dog' analogy when trying to convey the kind of effect the presence of the 'visitors' had upon him, by surmising, 'To an intelligence of sufficiently greater power, it may be that we would seem as obvious as animals seem to us – and we might feel as exposed as do some dogs when their masters stare into their eyes.'[22] That would seem to be it in a nutshell. Do we ask permission of our dogs for what we do to them? No, we presume a right because they 'belong' to us, they are our creature. After all we bred them for our benefit, didn't we? Such inferior creatures have no 'rights', only those privileges afforded to them by our ownership of them. If in our confrontation with the UFO phenomenon we find out what it's like when the boot is on the other foot, it couldn't happen to a nicer race. It would also explain why this phenomenon has always related to us from a position of god-like superiority; that is probably the only kind of interface possible between one man and his dog – if you get my metaphor.

As it was in the beginning, so it is now, and probably always will be. The one correlation that cannot apparently be countenanced by ufologists (ufologians would be a more accurate designation the way things are going), be they ETH proponents, earthlights adherents, psychic solutionists or just plain sceptics, is the undeniable interface flying saucery has with religion. It pleases them not when it is pointed out that the progress of ufology down the years parallels the development of religious movements. First came the New Revelation (spaceships above!) which was persecuted by adherents of the entrenched cosmological orthodoxies. Gradually, the study developed its own dogma, canonized a number of 'martyrs', was 'reformed' into 'new ufology', and finally broke into a number of autonomous 'sects' which were, in large measure, inimical to one another. As this was going on, almost imperceptibly, earlier religious revelations were being reinterpreted according to the gospel of ufology, until it was abundantly clear, except to a metaphysically myopic humankind, that the next inevitable step was for humanity to fall down and worship the *deus ex machina* of the skies. Perhaps the proposition is so inherently odious to us that the gut reaction of a latter-day resurgence of the original orthodoxy that seeks to make the Establishment (the American Establishment in particular) 'come clean' and admit that UFOs are spaceships, and that the creatures associated with them are therefore EBEs (extraterrestrial biological entities) was only to be expected. Unfortunately, even in this otherwise space-alien orientated area, there is no getting away from the religious undercurrent, because the alleged 'aliens' in Area 51 (a facility similar to Hangar 18) have allegedly begun to claim responsibility for a number of religious initiatives heretofore credited solely to the Will of God. According to Timothy Good, a champion of the orthodox ETH, Bob Lazar had sight of some 'briefing papers' in which it was stated that humankind was the product of periodic genetic tampering by 'aliens'. In a private interview conducted by George Knapp, Lazar apparently admitted that according to the information in the 'briefing papers', 'we were made by progressive corrections in evolution and that sort of thing'.[23] Interestingly, we could claim that we made the race of dogs that presently exists by means of progressive corrections in evolution. It is just a fancy way of describing the process of breeding. Even if, in our case, hands-on genetic engineering was involved, it is merely a matter of the degree of 'correction' utilized. Apparently, the 'aliens' also claimed to have 'genetically engineered' Jesus and sundry other (unspecified) religious leaders. Perhaps Hitler was one of them. As Bob Lazar apparently said, 'It is a tough thing to believe without proof.' But as Timothy Good's book goes on to reveal, Lazar also claimed that the papers he had seen included 'an extremely classified document dealing with religion, and it's extremely thick'.[24] He then asked, perhaps somewhat rhetorically, 'But why should there be any classified document dealing with religion?'[25] I presume for the very same reason that the Vatican has an extremely classified document dealing with a particular prophecy of the BVM at Fatima. According to the information in the briefing papers, the 'alien's' name for us is 'containers'. Lazar seemed to think that this must mean that our bodies are 'containers' for 'souls', especially since the information in the papers alleged that religion had been created so that there would be some rules and regulations to govern our conduct to prevent the 'containers' being damaged. This is an apparent paradox, because religion has been the cause of the greatest damage to 'containers' bar none. Perhaps the alleged 'aliens' actually called us 'retainers', and the rest is down to human error. Certainly 'retainer' would be the correct name for a being that was intended to be a 'civilized vassal'. Of course, the real point at issue is why aliens from space should display such an interest in, and familiarity with, our parochial tribal superstitions. Superior aliens, I suggest, would either exploit or ignore us depending on what they came to Earth to obtain. But what of creatures who were forced to share the planet with us because both our species were of the Earth? Having once experienced our inability to control our aggressive tendencies, they might seek to regain control of us by encouraging us to 'worship' them while they, using specimens aboard the starships deep in space at the time of the Cretaceous confrontation, were trying to breed our replacement free from the genetic defect that made us dangerous to know. Should they succeed, the much prophesied and long-awaited 'end of the world' might yet come about . . . at least for us. Considering the state of our planet, it is the least we deserve. With us gone for good, perhaps 'the peoples of Agharti will come up from their subterranean caverns to the surface of the earth'[26] and the dinosaurs will have regained what is rightfully theirs . . .

References

[1] *The Sirius Mystery*, Robert K. G. Temple (Futura, 1976).
[2] *Sun Songs*, ed. Raymond Van Over (Mentor Book, 1980).
[3] ibid.
[4] Temple, op. cit.
[5] ibid.
[6] *UFOs: The Psychic Solution*, Jacques Vallée (Panther Books, 1977).
[7] *Fatima: A Close Encounter of the Worst Kind?*, David Barclay (Mark Saunders Publications, 1987).
[8] ibid.
[9] 'Fire Down Below', David Barclay, *The Unknown*, July 1985.
[10] *Hitler's Secret Sciences*, Nigel Pennick (Neville Spearman, 1981).
[11] ibid.
[12] *The Morning of the Magicians*, Louis Pauwels and Jacques Bergier (Mayflower, 1971).
[13] *The Lost World of Agharti*, Alec Maclellan (Souvenir Press, 1982).
[14] ibid.
[15] Pauwels and Bergier, op. cit.
[16] *Operation Trojan Horse*, John A. Keel (Souvenir Press, 1971).
[17] ibid.
[18] Pauwels and Bergier, op. cit.
[19] *Mystery of the Ancients*, Eric and Craig Umland (Panther Books, 1976).
[20] *Communion*, Whitley Strieber (Arrow, 1988).
[21] ibid.
[22] ibid.
[23] *Alien Liaison*, Timothy Good (Arrow, 1992).
[24] ibid.
[25] ibid.
[26] Maclellan, op. cit.

CHAPTER 13
The Real Aliens?

AS THE world rushes headlong towards the twenty-first century, there still seem to be more questions than answers in ufology. So intimately is the UFO phenomenon apparently connected to all the other mysteries to which humankind is heir, I feel that it is almost inevitable that if science wants to solve it, it must inevitably solve the mystery of humankind first.

In this context, I consider the words 'I Believe' to be the most intellectually inept combination in the English language. It does not matter in what context they are used, be it sacred or secular, they usually signal the abandonment of argumentative impartiality for the emotional trenches of cherished belief systems. Take something as seemingly simple as our presence on this planet. It seems only logical to suppose that, as we are obviously here, then we must have got here somehow. Religion maintains that God made us. Science argues that natural selection made us. Both these views are beliefs, probably based on nothing more substantial than the unwarranted assumptions of their proponents, rather than expressions of demonstrable fact. In other words, both are dependent on 'belief systems'. Consequentially, they are due in large measure to the ego-related antagonisms such belief systems engender. The only contribution science and religion have so far made to the debate on the mystery of the origins of humankind is to confront each other in defence of their respective bodies of dogma.

At the time of writing, the prelates of palaeontology are apparently all agog over some four and a half million-year-old monkey bones recently unearthed in Ethiopia, without actually overcommitting themselves to the opinion they have allowed the media to imply that this fossil find is probably the remains of the much-sought-after evolutionary 'missing link'. But from past experience of the eventual fate of similar fossil 'finds', I take leave to doubt that the remains of one of my ancestors have been exhumed. While I would not deny the palaeontological probability that a plethora of ape-like individuals did indeed roam the world ages ago, I would argue that it is just as likely that these were the result of degenerative mutation caused by radiation-damaged genes, as the outcome of some, still largely hypothetical, impersonal process called 'evolution'. Regrettably, from the 'scientific' stand point in this matter, the premier proponent of 'evolution', Charles Darwin, was an amateur who:

> did not derive his theory from nature but rather superimposed a certain philosophical world-view on nature and then spent 20 years trying to gather the facts to make it stick.[1]

So, even though his intellectual heirs are still trying to make monkeys of us, I consider that the way is still left open for a more imaginative interpretation of what facts that are concerning our racial genesis.

Thankfully, I do not now have to have recourse to erudite experiments to prove that we, the human race, are radically different to all other primates living on the Earth at this time. All I now need to do is point out that:

> There are at least 312 listed physical traits that set us apart from our 'cousins'.[2]

and leave you to draw your own conclusions, while I point out the possibility that, because of these differences, to argue, on the basis of extant fossil evidence, that humankind is an 'evolved' anthropoid is about as sensible as arguing, from the 'evidence' of their respective rusting remains, that a Boeing 707 is merely an 'evolved' Cadillac Eldorado – both 'artefacts' having seats, doors, windows, wheels, and tailfins. If it were just a matter of superficial physical differences, as was the case with the species observed by Darwin in the Galapagos, I still might accept evolution as a possible factor in our development; but there is the matter of our brain and the incredible intellect it endows us with. In evolutionary terms, there was absolutely no need for it. In fact, present planetary trends affirm it is probably more of a hindrance than a help to survival. Interestingly, from what physical evidence there is, it would appear that we did not develop our intellect in some life-or-death evolutionary struggle to become the dominant species, but apparently appeared out of nowhere, peculiarly 'pre-adapted' in this way to live in the kind of world we have now created for ourselves. Apparently, no further 'evolutionary' modification has been necessary to equip the 'stone age hunter/gatherer' to invent and operate the increasingly ecocidal technology of the late twentieth century. This can only support the suspicion that 'evolution' is probably just another of those nineteenth-century non-scientific notions. Well, at least when applied to the Human Race it is, as Alfred Russell Wallace openly admitted, and even Darwin covertly recognized. Our brains were, and still are (we apparently still only use 10 per cent of their potential), developed far in excess of anything that can be explained on the basis of 'natural selection' which, according to Wallace, 'never over-endows a species beyond the demands of everyday existence'. So, if nature is not guilty, what unnatural act brought us into being? An act of God, as Wallace proposed, or something not quite so staggeringly supernatural?

In more ways than one, the individual who stares back at you from your bathroom mirror every morning is probably just as alien as the life form you have been led to believe drives around in flying saucers. Gaze deeply into its eyes and try to realize that you are not the biggest mistake that nature ever made, but more probably the descendant of a dog-like domesticated dinosaur. That we owe our existence to a process probably identical to the one that produced the domesticated mammalian canine is argued by the incredible variegation of individuals in the human race, and the fact that 'no other animal species varies as much in shape, size and colour except the dog, which man himself has domesticated'.[3] That the original wild stock from which we were bred was not mammalian is also ineluctably indicated by the decisive physical differences that set us apart from all contemporary mammalian development. The unique sexual hydraulics of the human male have already been mentioned, as has the hymen of the female. But, equally evidential of our non-mammalian origins is the fact that 'the fertilized human ovum attaching itself to the uterine wall is a distinct departure from the free-floating ova of all other earth creatures'.[4] Demonstrably, we are not mammals. But this would not necessarily make us dinosaurs . . . except for the surprising 'synchronicity' that 'since the dinosaurs, no other creature has been able to adapt so readily to extremes of heat, cold, drought and deluge'.[5] Circumstantial though it is, I suggest that all the evidence seems to point to the possibility of the human race being, among other things, a living dinosaur. So why has science not suggested this solution as a means to explaining why humankind does not conform to the requirements of Darwinian evolutionary theory, based as it is on the principle of natural selection?

Much of the difficulty that the modern scientific mentality has in coming to terms with the possibility that the human race might have existed during the days of the dinosaurs, and therefore probably is – by inference – itself a dinosaur, is due to the fact that it has not yet overcome the intellectual inertia imposed by the nineteenth-century geological 'doctrine' of 'uniformitarianism'. It proposes, 'Present continuity implies the improbability of past catastrophism and violence of change, either in the lifeless or in the living world.'[6] As the theory of evolution is based on the doctrine of uniformitarianism, it makes it impossible for conventional palaeontologists to consider the possibility of atomic Armageddon in antiquity. Their hypothesizing is ham-strung by the geologists' absolutist assumption of incredibly extended spans of time to explain the Earth changes evident in the geological record. Thus the science of palaeontology is caught between a rock and a hard place when trying to determine 'scientifically' the actual genesis of humankind from fossil evidence. To compound this cosmological confusion, the science of geology, at its inception, was called upon to confound the claims of religious fundamentalism which maintained that the Earth was only 4,000 or so years old. And so it came to pass that the intellectual initiative necessary to undermine the insupportable beliefs of religious fundamentalism, while at the same time accommodating the equally insupportable beliefs of uniformitarianism, produced yet another scientific shibboleth for the intellectually intransigent to cower behind, even to the present day. This ensured that the one viable proposition not given the consideration it deserved was that the Earth, while not so young as biblical fundamentalism believed it to be, might not be quite as old as conventional geology makes it out to be by ignoring the very real possibility that 'nearly all of the dating methods that were devised have been faulty, not because of faulty conception or sloppy application, but because they were based on unwarranted assumptions'.[7] Arguing intransigently from unwarranted assumptions in favour of insupportable absolutes is the hallmark of a belief system – be it found in theology, cosmology, palaeontology, geology or ufology – thinking any conclusions arrived at by such means cannot be relied upon and should be discarded rather than defended. The inescapable logic of the possibility of errors in extant dating strategies is that, if all previous assumptions regarding the dating of events on planet Earth have been found wanting, then 'the latest assumptions may also prove defective'.[8] In which case, the vast panoply of prehistoric events, up to and including the genesis of humankind, probably remain effectively undated. This makes even more significant those geological 'erratics' that indicate humankind and the dinosaurs probably existed contemporaneously prior to the Cretaceous calamity. If true, would this explain our race's ongoing interest in creatures that allegedly disappeared from the face of the earth aeons before Pithecanthropus was so much as an itch in the loins of some problematical pro-simian? Almost certainly, the public response to the latest cinematographic depiction of the dinosaurs, Spielberg's *Jurassic Park* – unequivocally indicates that something in our 'collective unconscious' is strangely stirred by the thought of being confronted by living representatives of this long-vanished race of leviathans.

So, given the very real shortcomings of the theory of evolution as it presently applies to humankind, and dependent as it is on the validity of the questionable hypothesis of uniformitarianism, is it possible that humankind really is *not* a natural product of this planet, but must be considered alien to the mammalian world in which it now finds itself trapped? At the moment, the only people who might answer with a qualified 'Yes!' are the proponents of sundry versions of the ancient astronaut hypothesis, as pioneered by von Daniken, who stated quite categorically: 'I postulate that unknown beings created human intelligence by a deliberate artificial mutation.'[9] His sentiments are echoed almost exactly by others, notably Max Flindt, author of *On Tiptoe Beyond Darwin*, who, with renowned UFO and space expert Otto Binder, proposed: 'Mankind on earth may have had superintelligent ancestors.'[10] Even an ex-NASA employee, Maurice Chatelain, unable to accept the conventional explanations for humankind's 'sudden' acquisition of sophisticated knowledge in antiquity, had to ask: 'Can anyone really think that all that fantastic knowledge in astronomy, mathematics, geodesy, and many other sciences was acquired by mankind without outside help?'[11] The solution that most 'ancient astronaut' adherents propose to the evolutionary mystery posed by the existence of humankind is that we *must* be some kind of hybrid being. I agree. But a cross between half-wit hominid and superintelligent spaceman? You cannot be serious! Those who subscribe to this solution seem unable to realize that it only works from the stand point of human chauvinism. So, while I do not disagree that we probably are the product of genetic tampering, I cannot accept that 'extra-terrestrials ennobled man "in their own image"'.[12] In the first place, it is unlikely that exploring extraterrestrials would take time out to 'ennoble' a rather smelly and stupid simian – for any reason. In the second place, why should it be assumed that only 'advanced' extra-terrestrials would be able to engage in such pursuits anyway? What about a home-grown superior species – like an intelligent dinosaur?

Assuming, for the sake of argument, that a bipedal being much like ourselves actually did evolve from dinosaur stock during the 150 million or so years that the species existed on the Earth, what reason might such a creature have had for breeding humankind from one of the wild dinosaur types that existed during that time? Probably the very same reasons which led us, in our turn, to domesticate and breed dogs. The real trouble, from all our points of view, probably only started when the dinosaur civilization reached the point where experiments involving genetic engineering, including the splicing of their genes into various animals, became feasible – just as we, in our turn, are beginning to do today. I can only suppose that it must have seemed like a good idea at the time for the intelligent dinosaurs to 'create humankind in their own image' and so produce a self-replicating biological servomechanism to take the strain out of living. The story of what actually happened has been so garbled by transmission through time by word of mouth before it was written down (so ecclesiastical empire builders could tamper with it further), that it is surprising that any of it is still recognizable in the mythologies of the world. But it is. Many cultural mythologies, each in their own way, indicate that humankind was probably bred in much the same fashion as we have bred dogs, and for the same reasons. (To digress inconsequentially, I for one have been perennially piqued by the fact that the word 'dog' is a reversal of the word 'god', and have often wondered if in this odd coincidence some kind of Freudian slip was showing.) Everything probably went well up to the point when intelligent dinosaur genes were spliced into the human race in order to produce a being that would be capable of doing more than just bark (metaphorically?) at intruders. Our dinosaur breeders probably thought that the finished product would combine the desired dog-like qualities of loyalty, adulation, obedience, etc. with an enhanced capability for performing ever more complicated tasks. Perhaps we did – at first – but then someone went a step too far, introduced a comparable human female into the situation, and things went wrong . . . for all of us. Any attempt at a detailed reconstruction of the conflict that brought an end to the 'golden age', when we walked in the 'garden' with our 'creator', is best left to the cosmologists, geologists and palaeontologists of the future who, hopefully, will not labour under the intellectual burdens bequeathed to the present generation by the overweening atheistic anthropocentricism of an age that thought it knew most of the answers. In fact, it did not even know the questions! For the purposes of this present work, it should be sufficient to demonstrate that Genesis is an accurate enough account of the seminal event that turned us from being a faithful dog into a demonic hound of the Baskervilles that effectively bit the hand that bred it.

There is little doubt that the Genesis narrative is a cosmological compendium drawn from an immeasurably older and much more widespread mythology, because 'the Biblical story (or allegory) of Adam and Eve is strangely repeated in the sacred books and traditions of other religions and peoples'.[13] The probability is that, in plagiarizing the Edenic myth from earlier sources, which themselves probably derived from even earlier verbal traditions, 'The scribes who attempted to put together the encyclopedia of history we call the Bible made some progress in their own way and according to their understanding.'[14] And because their understanding was limited, the account they compiled as an exercise in monodeific propaganda still has the ring of truth, providing you lay aside any preconceptions about the God of the

Universe being some kind of market gardener on planet Earth. What the Genesis narrative is actually saying is that at some point in time the human race was called into being as a kind of 'guard dog' by a life form that gave every evidence of being both fallible and autocratic. The argument in favour of the creation myth in Genesis being an accurate, if inevitably 'mythologized', record of events is enhanced by the fact that those who compiled it, ostensibly with the intention of attributing 'creation' to their tribal god, failed to understand how their narrative was replete with the kind of inference, incident and dialogue that practically proved that, whoever the 'Lord God' of the Genesis account was, he was *not* the Universal Creator, nor was he alone. In style, even when translated into English, the Genesis narrative gives the impression that it could be a badly understood and inexpertly condensed account of events that occurred over a lengthy period. Whether or not 'Adam', 'Eve' and 'God' were actual individuals or personificiations of their particular kind is unclear, but that does not matter. What matters is that the narrative makes it clear that the human race rebelled against the ones who bred it. In spite of what the Genesis narrative maintains, it is more than probable that this rebellion had nothing whatsoever to do with 'Eve' eating apples. Writing about 'eating the fruit of the tree of Knowledge' was just a poetic way of saying somebody learned something. In the 'garden of Eden' humankind apparently learned to tell the difference between 'Good' and 'Evil'. In reality, there are no such things as 'Good' and Evil', because everything is relative and depends on viewpoint. However, once you are able to make this determination between 'Good and Evil', subjective though it might be, you are in a position to assess if any situation you are in is 'good' for you or not. Ergo, when the 'Lord God' of the Edenic myth exclaimed, 'Behold the man has become as one of us to know good and evil,'[15] he was probably only acknowledging the fact that our 'first parents' had somehow sussed out that they were being exploited by him, and they were determined to have no more of it. This, from the point of view of the 'Lord God', was *bad*. This act of 'disobedience' was something far more anarchistic than just poor old Adam pulling on a pair of designer fig leaves to 'cover his nakedness'. It inevitably possessed the potential to escalate out of control and be *really bad* for whoever the 'us' was that humankind had 'become like'. This can be deduced from the fact that the 'Lord God' of Eden obviously feared the consequences should humankind, now able to differentiate between 'Good and Evil', arrive at the inevitable conclusion that physical immortality is very good indeed, and so 'put forth his hand and take also from the tree of life, and eat, and live forever'.[16] The comment in the Bible that for this reason 'the Lord God sent him [humankind] forth from the Garden of Eden'[17] probably glosses over a conflict that put paid to the intelligent dinosaurs' dreams of dominion, and reduced human-kind to an amnesiac android with a guilt complex. Clearly, something of seminal significance for our race took place in antiquity in the 'garden of Eden', but was it what we have been led to believe by conventional theology? Surely, you still don't seriously believe that an Almighty and Omnipotent Universal Creator (if He exists at all) would react in the way described in Genesis just because a bipedal being He modelled out of clay and then stuck on a mudball in the middle of nowhere got a bit shirty about its lot in life, do you? Or, as geology and palaeontology would have you believe, that the human adventure on Earth can be explained as 'a product of random events, chance mutations, and individually unlikely steps',[18] a kind of culmination of cosmological coincidences?

It might surprise you to learn that it does not matter what you believe, because human belief systems have never been a reliable yardstick with which to measure reality. The reason that I reluctantly abandoned the increasingly popular paradigm of 'space aliens' as a solution to the UFO-entity mystery is primarily because:

> It is demonstrable from many sources that the phenomenon that has come to be known in this latter half of the twentieth century as 'UFOs' has been endemic throughout history.[19]

but also because, due to the UFO entities' documented overfamiliarity with our anthropocentric parochial cosmologies:

> It can only be that the UFO phenomenon has an interface with human society as it developed on this planet.[20]

Putting it bluntly, I strongly suspect 'they' have been here too long and know too damn much about us to be space aliens. On top of this, there are the complications of the UFO–religion correlation to explain, as well as the alleged clandestine impregnation of human females by ufonauts – and that is before you get to the so-called 'psychic' aspects of the overall enigma. Although there have been many excellent hypotheses evolved to meet the challenge, none of them has been inclusive and each has usually left one or more aspects of the phenomenon to go begging.

Although mammals apparently got their evolutionary start in the Triassic period, before the dinosaurs, the subsequent dinosaur development completely suppressed them. What, if anything, could have been the secret of the dinosaurs' success? Perhaps the species was naturally 'psychic' so that to a greater or lesser degree individual dinosaurs were telepathic, telekinetic, etc. Any 'intelligent dinosaur' evolving from these beginnings would probably possess 'psychic' talents that would enable it to manipulate its environment in ways presently inconceivable to us. The kind of technology such a race would develop would have aspects incomprehensible to creatures less psychically gifted. Yet, if this race were so superior, it still chose to ally itself with the forebears of humankind in much the same way that we allied ourselves with the wild forebears of dogs. The partnership must have been just as successful as the one we presently have with dogs, perhaps even more so, otherwise the race would never have considered 'breeding' us into a being 'in their own image'. Because, in nature, life forms always act out of self-interest, and because I consider it of high probability that, racially, we are a hybrid of some sort, I have to consider this 'dinosaur breeding programme' as being more feasible than the one presuming that unbelievably humanoid aliens from elsewhere altruistically advanced us up the terrestrial food chain. In addition to which:

> The hoary science-fiction standby of the sexual love between a human being and an inhabitant of another planet ignores, in the most fundamental sense, the biological realities.[23]

Which inevitably means that:

> The category of contact story, now quite fashionable in some UFO enthusiast circles, of sexual contact between human and

saucerian . . . must be relegated to the realm of improbable fantasy.[24]

Even so, this does not automatically mean that the human race cannot be a genetically engineered hybrid. The evidence indicating the probability of human hybridization is not the visible variegation between individuals, nor even our unmammalian sexual apparatus, but the fact that only humankind, of all the animals on Earth, falls victim to the mental illness called schizophrenia, literally 'split mind'. Considering that it is a fairly common form of human mental illness, the symptoms of which were known and described well before this century, it seems surprising that 'what actually causes schizophrenia is one of the major mysteries of medicine.'[21] Can the reason for this be because those treating the disease are thinking in terms of a theory of evolution that makes humankind an advanced but entirely holistic hominid descendant, when in fact he is more likely to be the product of an experiment in ill-advised genetic splicing? In which case, the schizophrenic condition in which the patient displays 'evidence of being only partly a rational human being . . . and becomes a personality of dual nature'[22] becomes medically explicable as a 'split' into the two incompatible halves of 'domesticated dog-like dinosaur' and 'superior intelligent dinosaur'. If this 'split mind' condition is evidence of the suspected hybridization of humanity, can it explain the onset of schizophrenia in terms of a 'rejection' of the intrusive genetic material in the same way as 'rejection' of transplanted organs cause physical symptoms in the recipient? It might be interesting to see what progress the psychiatric professionals might make using this 'model' as a means to understand this puzzling illness.

By accepting at face value the evidence for our unnatural genesis as a race, is it now possible to deduce why we were 'bred' in this way? Folklore, religious myth, and pagan legend all agree, and our documented progress through history proclaims it. Waging war has been the human obsession to which all our other talents have been subjugated. It, therefore, seems a safe bet that when our breeders spliced their own superior genetic material into ours, their intention was to turn us into their dogs of war. It was the biggest mistake they ever made. The genetic 'transplant' did not take in the way expected, and before our breeders realized that they had put the implements of insurrection into the hands of an emotionally immature being, the human race rebelled. That this cataclysmic lesson left a lasting impression on those who bred us to be their slaves is argued by the fact that their successors, for all their ufological meddling, apparently still fear us. It was this aspect of his abduction that took Whitley Strieber by surprise, because from their overt behaviour towards him he clearly got the impression that 'they not only feared me, they seemed in awe of me.'[25] Well, so would you be if you knew you were tampering with a member of the race whose ancestors had practically wiped yours off the face of the Earth. They (and also, I strongly suspect, certain members of the human race) must know that the issue between us has not been satisfactorily settled.

According to the documentary programme *Viewpoint*, screened on Tuesday 28 April 1992, the acquisition of physical immortality is just around the temporal corner. In a tie-in article by Alison Brewer in the 25 April–1 May issue of the *TV Times*, it is revealed that American scientist Dr Mike West has discovered that, as individual organisms, we are seemingly 'programmed' to self-destruct (die) once we are past our procreationary peak. Because of his researches into the human-ageing process, Dr West maintains that the human organism seems built to be immortal except that 'nature' has apparently 'built in' a self-destruct mechanism in the form of homicidal enzymes. In view of the evidence that indicates that humankind was 'made' rather than 'evolved', I can only conclude that this means that the 'Lord God' of Eden was familiar with the concept of 'planned obsolescence'. This might explain his anger and anxiety, as graphically described in Genesis, when he was confronted by his creatures' new found perspicacity. He knew this unexpected acquisition would probably lead to 'Adam and Eve' discovering what he had done to them, and so inevitably provoke them into trying to 'take also from the tree of life, and eat, and live forever'. If they were successful in the endeavour, it would make them (and by inference the entire human race) the equal of their makers. In this context, it can only be suspected of being 'synchronous' that the entity enigma, with its abductions, impregnations, and threats of approaching Armageddons, should come to prominence at a time when humankind's medical science is fast approaching the point where the second apple of Eden (the one that will make humankind immortal) will be well within its grasp. Already, Dr West has allegedly discovered a means to reverse the ageing process, and has in his laboratory samples of human skin tissue, brain cells and cartilage which he has made immortal. Only the final step – to refine the process so that it can be applied to the human organism as a whole – still awaits. Apparently this problem is being tackled by research funded to the tune of one billion dollars. Who said there are some things that money cannot buy?

If, according to Genesis, it was the possibility of humankind becoming immortal that caused all the contention in the first place, I wonder what the gods of Eden are going to do about it this time? If they are still around, that is. Because of the manifestations of the UFO phenomenon, I strongly suspect they are. So, if anything is going to happen, now seems like as good a time as any.

References

[1] *Mankind – Child of the Stars*, Max H. Flindt and Otto O. Binder (Fawcett, 1974).

[2] *World Atlas of Mysteries*, Francis Hitching (Pan, 1981).

[3] ibid.

[4] *Flying Saucers Are Watching Us*, Otto O. Binder (Belmont Productions, 1968).

[5] Hitching, op. cit.

[6] *Subdue the Earth*, Ralph Franklin Walworth and Geoffrey Walworth Sjostrom (Granada, 1980).

[7] ibid.

[8] ibid.

[9] *According to the Evidence*, Erich von Daniken (Corgi, 1978).

[10] Flindt and Binder, op. cit.

[11] *Our Ancestors Came From Outer Space*, Maurice Chatelain (Dell, 1979).

[12] von Daniken, op. cit.

[13] Binder, op. cit.

[14] 'A Funny Thing Happened (on the way to extinction)', C. A. O'Conner, *The UFO Debate*, Vol. 2, No. 3.

[15] Genesis 4: 22–23.

[16] ibid.

[17] ibid.

[18] *The Cosmic Connection*, Carl Sagan (Coronet, 1975).

[19] *UFOs: The Final Answer?*, ed. David Barclay and Therese Marie Barclay (Blandford, 1993).

[20] ibid.

[21] Flindt and Binder, op. cit.
[22] ibid.
[23] Sagan, op. cit.
[24] ibid.
[25] *Communion*, Whitley Strieber (Arrow, 1988).

Index

Newmarket Public Library